Robert Winston

What goes on in my HEAD?

A DORLING KINDERSLEY BOOK

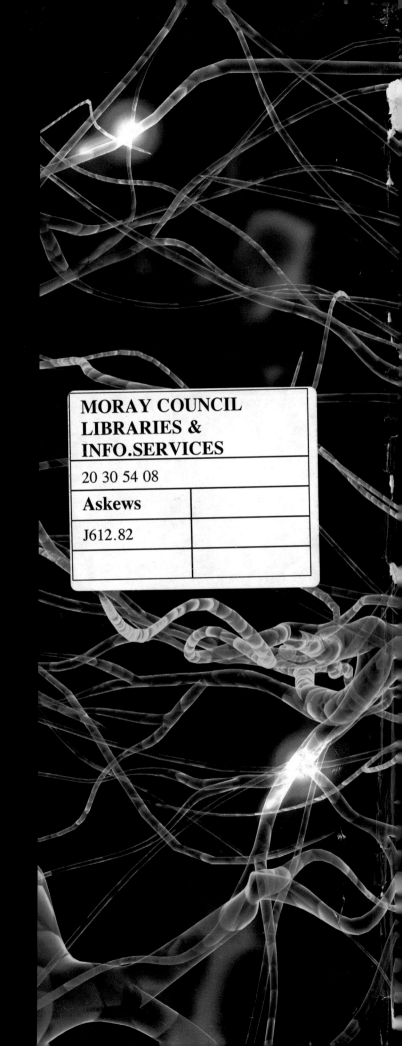

LONDON, NEW YORK, MUNICH,
MELBOURNE, and DELHI

Senior Editor Ben Morgan
Senior Designers Claire Patané, Rachael Grady
Editors Alexander Cox, Wendy Horobin, Rob Houston,
Fleur Star, Lee Wilson, Jessamy Wood, Chris Woodford
Designers Karen Hood, Sadie Thomas, Lauren Rosier,
Sonia Whillock-Moore

Picture researcher Liz Moore
Production editor Siu Yin Chan
Production controller Claire Pearson
Jacket editor Matilda Gollon
Publishing manager Bridget Giles
Art director Martin Wilson
Creative director Jane Bull
Publisher Mary Ling

Consultant Dr Sarah-Jayne Blakemore

First published in Great Britain in 2010 by
Dorling Kindersley Limited
80 Strand, London WC2R 0RL

Copyright © 2010 Dorling Kindersley Limited
A Penguin Company

2 4 6 8 10 9 7 5 3 1
177960 – 06/2010

A CIP catalogue record for this book
is available from the British Library.

ISBN: 978-1-40535-373-1

Colour reproduction by Media Development and Printing Ltd, UK
Printed and bound in Slovakia by Tlaciarne BB s.r.o.

Jacket images: Front: **Corbis:** Image Source ftl (jigsaw piece); moodboard fcr (chess
pieces); Marc Rimmer c (fish); Ken Seet clb (family); Visuals Unlimited (brain);
Dorling Kindersley: Robert L. Braun – modelmaker fcra (dinosaur); The National
Birds of Prey Centre, Gloucestershire crb (kestrel); Simon Rawles / Football School
Reader at Whittington Park, London cla (boy); Satellite Imagemap / 1996-23
Planetary Visions fcla (earth); **NASA:** JPL-Caltech / STScI fcr (supernova); **Science
Photo Library:** TEK Image cl (monitor); Emmeline Watkins cr (radio).
Back: **Corbis:** Image Source ftl; **Science Photo Library:** Mehau Kulyk cl, cr

Discover more at
www.dk.com

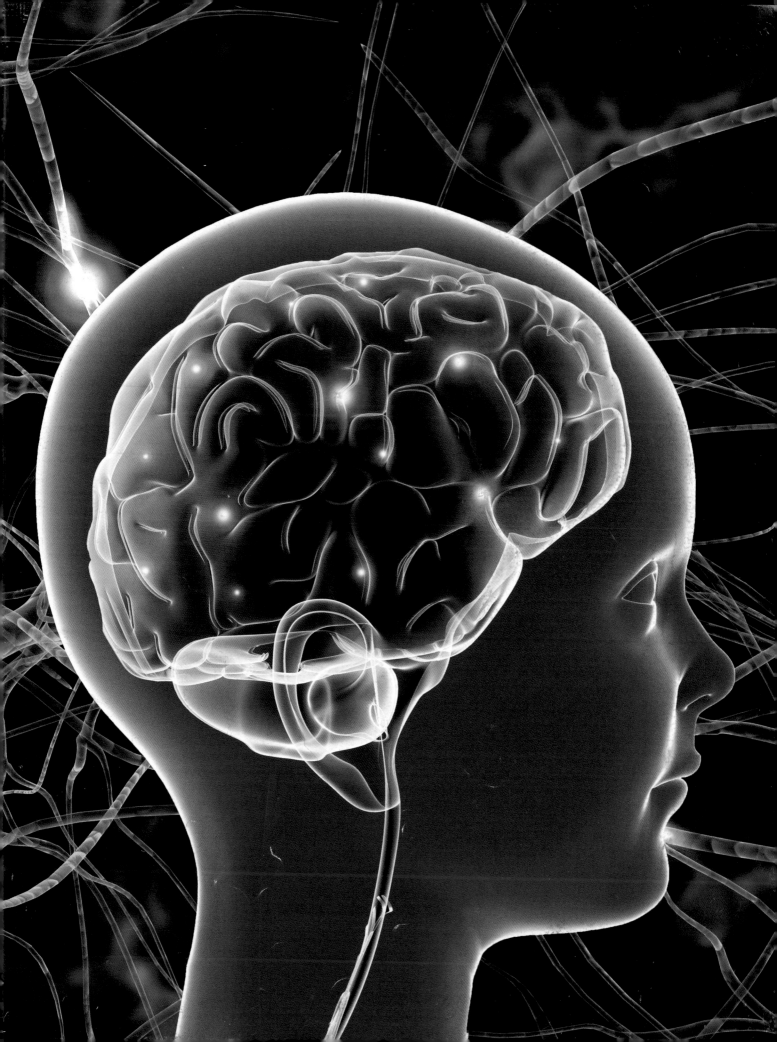

The **BRAIN** is the most *amazing*

It weighs roughly 1400 grams (3 lbs) — little more than a medium-sized bag of sugar — and is about the size of a cauliflower.

It looks a bit like a yellowish, rubbery **fungus** covered with a few TINY red blood vessels. Yet the **HUMAN BRAIN** is the most *complicated object in the universe* — and each person's brain is **UNIQUE**.

It is the centre of where we think, ***love**, **laugh**,* and **LEARN**, and it controls the rest of our body. So it's not surprising that it is *delicate* too, which is why it is protected by the skull and why we need to **LOOK AFTER IT.**

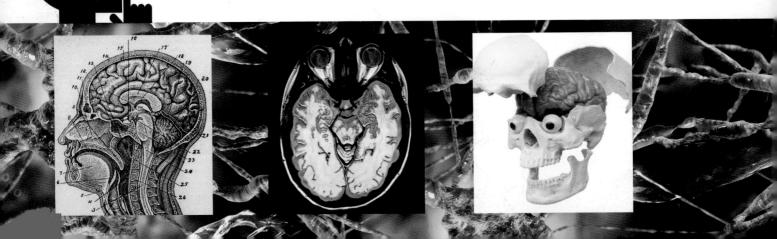

organ in the human body – and the most mysterious.

Inside each brain is a *vast number* of tiny cells, the most important of which are the ***neurons*** – spindly, wire-like cells that pass electrical signals to other neurons. There are roughly **100 BILLION** of these in the brain, and each may be connected to up to 10,000 others.

Every second – even when we sleep – **TRILLIONS** of electrical signals speed among our neurons, weaving *infinitely tangled paths* through the most complex network we know.

It is THE MIRACLE of EVOLUTION, making each of us what we are.

PROFESSOR ROBERT WINSTON

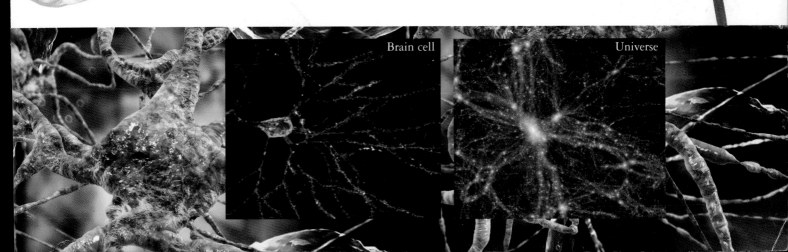

Brain cell

Universe

CONTENTS

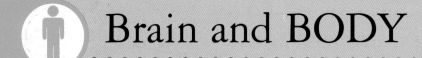

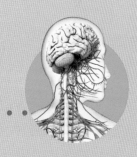

 INTRODUCING *the brain*

For centuries, people thought the heart or soul were where thoughts and feelings came from and regarded the brain as *useless gunk*. Thanks to a few gruesome discoveries, the truth about that mysterious gunk in our heads slowly began to emerge. Today, we know more about the brain than ever, yet it remains a *riddle wrapped in a mystery*. It's the very organ we use to understand itself, yet it's the only organ we don't *really understand* – and perhaps never will.

Discovering the BRAIN

If it weren't for scientists and about 8500 years of history, you might not even know you had a brain in your head. From realizing we have a brain . . .

I'm the greatest!

Ancient Egyptians gave the brain a name but otherwise had little time for it. Before making a mummy from a dead body, they'd carefully preserve its heart. But the brain was scraped out through the nostrils and chucked away.

What's that *smell?*

Herophilus, a Greek doctor, kicked off the science of anatomy by prising open dead bodies and sketching what he found inside. After making detailed studies of the eye and nerves, he realized the brain was the body's control centre.

| 6500 BCE | 1077 BCE | 400 BCE | 300 BCE | 0 |

Trepanning was boring old brain surgery – literally. Used from the Stone Age onwards, it involved drilling holes in the skull, more or less at random. It was used to "treat" many types of illness from mild headaches to out-and-out madness.

I needed that like a hole in the head...

Aristotle, a Greek thinker, was the world's first great scientist, but he had some wacky ideas about the brain. He thought the heart was in charge of our emotions, while the brain was little more than a radiator that stopped the body overheating.

. . . to figuring out precisely what this squidgy, head-mounted computer actually does has been a long and slow but fascinating process.

Andreas Vesalius gave us the
first detailed drawings of the brain. One of the sketches was from a murderer who'd been hanged and beheaded. As if that wasn't enough, Vesalius chopped up his body in public, reassembling the bones later for display at the local university.

Phineas Gage was a hard-
working and reliable railway worker until an accident at work blew a metal spike through the front of his brain. Suddenly he became rude, careless, and aggressive. This famous case revealed how damage to the brain's frontal lobe can cause a dramatic change in someone's character.

That's given me a headache!

1543   1637   1848 1850

The first psychology laboratory, in Germany, 1879.

René Descartes was
a French philosopher who liked to scribble away in bed until noon. His famous idea was that the mind and body were totally separate things that could, nevertheless, work together. He's best remembered for saying "I think therefore I am".

Shh, I'm thinking!

Hermann von Helmholtz
helped make psychology into a science. His experiments on how people see colours and hear sounds were the first scientific studies of perception. Wilhelm Wundt built on his work to found experimental psychology (studying behaviour using scientific methods).

Paul Broca was a French doctor who discovered where speech is produced in the brain. One of his patients was nicknamed "Tan" because that was the only word he could say. When Tan died, Broca examined his brain and found damage to the left front side. Broca realized the damaged bit (now called Broca's area) must be involved in moving the mouth to form words. This was the first time anyone had really tried to find which bits of the brain did what.

Tan, tan tan, tan!

Sigmund Freud, a hugely influential Austrian doctor, believed mental problems could be traced back to experiences in childhood. According to Freud, people are driven by "unconscious" forces they aren't aware of, except in dreams and nightmares. Freud invented a treatment called psychoanalysis, where patients lay back on a cosy couch and moaned about their life while the analyst listened patiently, explained what was wrong, then gave them a huge bill. Some of Freud's ideas have now fallen out of favour for being unscientific, but he still regarded as a great thinker.

Tell me about your childhood...

1861 1870   1900   1914

Dr Eduard Hitzig, a German neurologist, carried out shocking experiments on injured soldiers. When he poked a tiny electric needle into their brains, he noticed the soldier's body jerked about. Repeating the experiment on dogs, he found he could move different parts of a dog's body by poking different bits of its brain. Prodding the left side of the brain made the right side of the body jerk, and vice-versa.

Left brain controls right side of body

Right brain controls left side

Henry Dale, a British scientist, discovered neurotransmitters (chemicals that relay signals between brain cells) in 1914. As a student Dale took part in public experiments on live animals that led to protests about cruelty. Animal experiments, which have led to many important discoveries about the brain, are now more strictly controlled to minimize suffering.

Gordon Holmes was an Irish doctor who specialized in studying damage to the rear part of the brain, including the cerebellum and brain stem. By examining the head wounds of over 2000 soldiers in the First World War, Holmes reached the conclusion that we see things in an area at the back of the brain that we now call the **visual cortex**.

I can see clearly now.

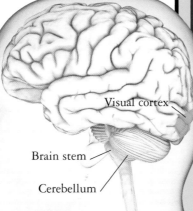

Visual cortex

Brain stem

Cerebellum

Lobotomies were a drastic kind of brain surgery, popular from the 1930s to the 1950s, intended to help people with mental illness or brain diseases such as epilepsy. The operation involved cutting the connections between the frontal lobe (a part of the brain vital for careful thinking) and the rest of the brain. It was quick and easy and could be done by hammering a knife into the brain through the eye socket. Although it often cured the patient's symptoms, it also caused unwanted changes in personality, and many doctors considered the operation barbaric. Thousands of people had lobotomies until the early 1970s, when newly invented drugs provided alternative treatments. Lobotomies are still carried out today, but much less frequently.

1919   1920   1934   1938

Electroencephalography is the detection and recording of "brain waves" – electrical waves from the brain – using an instrument worn on the head. Brain waves were first properly studied by Hans Berger, a German scientist who thought they might shed light on telepathy.

Burrhus Frederic Skinner, an American psychologist, thought we could understand how animals (including humans) behave without worrying too much about the brain. Called behaviourism, the theory was that animals do things because they're given rewards or punishments. This idea dominated psychology for years and put many scientists off studying the brain until the 1960s.

I smell a rat...

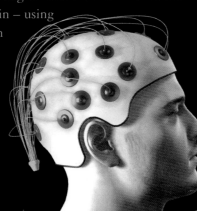

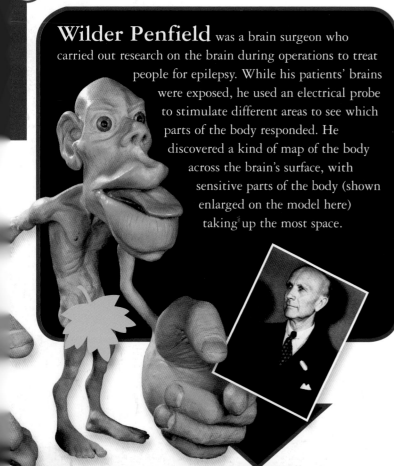

Wilder Penfield was a brain surgeon who carried out research on the brain during operations to treat people for epilepsy. While his patients' brains were exposed, he used an electrical probe to stimulate different areas to see which parts of the body responded. He discovered a kind of map of the body across the brain's surface, with sensitive parts of the body (shown enlarged on the model here) taking up the most space.

Cognitive psychology was a new way of studying the brain that took off in the 1960s. Until the 1960s, psychologists had studied behaviour and ignored what went on inside the brain. Now the psychologists began trying to figure out the brain's inner workings. They thought of the brain as a machine following simple rules that were programmed into it. The aim of cognitive psychology was to reveal the hidden rules underlying language, vision, memory, and other mental processes.

Whirr, whirr, click...

1951 1953   1960s

Who am *I?*

Henry Molaison
(known as "H.M.") had the world's most exhaustively studied bonce. After undergoing brain surgery to cure his epilepsy in 1953, he could no longer remember new things. He spent his remaining years as a patient, helping scientists to unravel the mysteries of memory.

Jose Delgado invented the first radio-controlled brain, in 1964. After sticking an electronic implant in a bull's brain, he stepped into a ring with an electronic controller and waited for the bull to charge him. Then he calmly pressed a button, zapped the bull, and brought it to a screeching halt.

I don't know if I'm coming or going.

Roger Sperry studied people who'd had surgery to separate the left and right halves of the brain – a last-resort cure for epilepsy. This drastic operation resulted in two "selves" controlling different parts of the body and sometimes disagreeing with one another!

"The great pleasure and feeling in my right brain is more than my left brain can find the words to tell you."

Neuroscience is the modern term for the scientific study of the brain. Neuroscientists think of brain cells (neurons) as electrical components that connect together to form complicated circuits. Neuroscience involves bits and pieces of many different areas of science, from biology and medicine to maths and computer science.

Neuroscience is all about being well-connected!

1970s   1980s   1995

Brain scans made it possible to look into the brain without smashing open the skull. This was great news for doctors (and for patients!) as it made detecting and treating illnesses such as brain tumours much easier. Scientists also began using brain scanners to see which bits of the healthy brain are most active when people do all sorts of tasks from reading books to seeing someone smile.

Mirror neurons, which might enable us to understand each other's behaviour and feelings, are among many exciting new discoveries being made in brain science. But lots of big questions remain, such as what sleep is for, how genes program the brain, how the brain changes through life, and how brain changes cause mental illness.

Why have a BRAIN?

You might *think* you can't survive without a brain, but MANY ANIMALS FARE PERFECTLY WELL WITHOUT ONE, and nobody has found so much as a nerve, let alone a brain, in a plant or a micoorganism. So what is the point of brains? And why are human brains so huge that they use up a fifth of our body's energy?

These have no brains

YUM YUM

PLANTS

While animals tend to lead active lives, moving around and exploring the world, plants spend their lives rooted to one spot. As a result, they don't need sophisticated sense organs or rapid reactions, so plants have no nervous system. And because they have no nervous system, they have no brain. Even so, plants can sense and respond to things. They can detect light and grow towards it, for instance, though their movement is usually so slow that we barely notice it.

Couch potato

Some sea animals spend their lives rooted to one spot, a bit like plants, and so have no need for a brain. A sea anemone is a brainless animal that lives stuck to a rock, waving its sticky tentacles to catch flood particles drifting by in the water. Although it has no brain, a simple network of nerves coordinates its movements and enables it to scrunch up into a ball if anything disturbs it.

????

NO HEAD, NO BRAIN

Starfish, sea urchins, jellyfish, and other headless animals don't think anything because they have no brain at all. They do not have a front end or a left or a right side. When they move, left is just as good as right or backwards – it makes no difference to their body direction. They have nerves, but like those of sea anemones, the nerves form a simple network spread throughout their body – nowhere are they bunched into a brainlike bulge.

Beginnings of brains

Animals with heads

Perhaps 1 billion years ago, worm-like animals began moving purposefully, with one part of their body – their front end, or head – leading the way. As they evolved and became better explorers, their eyes and other sense organs clustered on the head, because it was good to get sensations (food, danger, light, saltiness) as early as possible. It was convenient to have a bundle of nerves there, in the head, to analyse all the sense information that was pouring in. That bundle became a brain and the worms evolved into every animal with a front end alive today.

Which brain is in charge?

Octopuses are surprisingly clever, but they don't have a single, large brain. They do have a main brain, but two-thirds of their brain cells are spread out into their tentacles, making, in a way, a total of nine brains. With its own mini-brain, each of the octopus's arms works fairly independently without having to report back to the main brain. So the octopus doesn't get direct feedback from its arms and cannot "feel" where they are — that's the arm's job. The only way an octopus is completely aware of what its arms are doing is actually to look at them.

These animals have brains

A word on the wise

An owl has a big brain by bird standards, but this does not make it wise. The largest parts of its brain are those used for processing vision and hearing from its excellent eyes and ears, and for the precise movements of flying. It doesn't learn very much. Its brain usually acts automatically by instinct, following pre-programmed patterns of preening, sleeping, and feeding its chicks when they beg for food.

> THEN DO YOU KNOW WHAT SHE SAID TO ME?

> UNBELIEVABLE!

> I act on my instincts, a bit like an owl does, but I'm a cut above the average bird-brain. My mammal brain is much bigger than a bird-brain and is much better at learning new skills. Instead of relying so much on pre-installed software (instinct), my brain gets continual upgrades while I'm growing up and learning how to play, fight, hunt, climb, and survive.

BIG-BRAINED GOSSIPS

Humans brains are six times larger than those of similar-sized mammals. Why so big? Like other primates (monkeys, apes, and relatives), we live in social groups, and it pays to get on, socially. Gelada baboons have the biggest social groups in nature and spend 40 per cent of their lives grooming one another, nurturing their social bonds. Like humans, they have a huge frontal lobe — the thinking part of the brain. Perhaps humans have big brains because it takes brainpower to keep track of relationships with many other intelligent, unpredictable beings. Some experts think human gossiping evolved from grooming. Gossipers, like groomers, bond with one another, but they also get useful information about other people.

Brain *bits*

Push your fists tightly together – that's how big your brain is. And just like a pair of fists, **your brain is divided into two equal halves** and has a **knobbly, folded** surface. The surface is the part of the brain that makes humans clever.

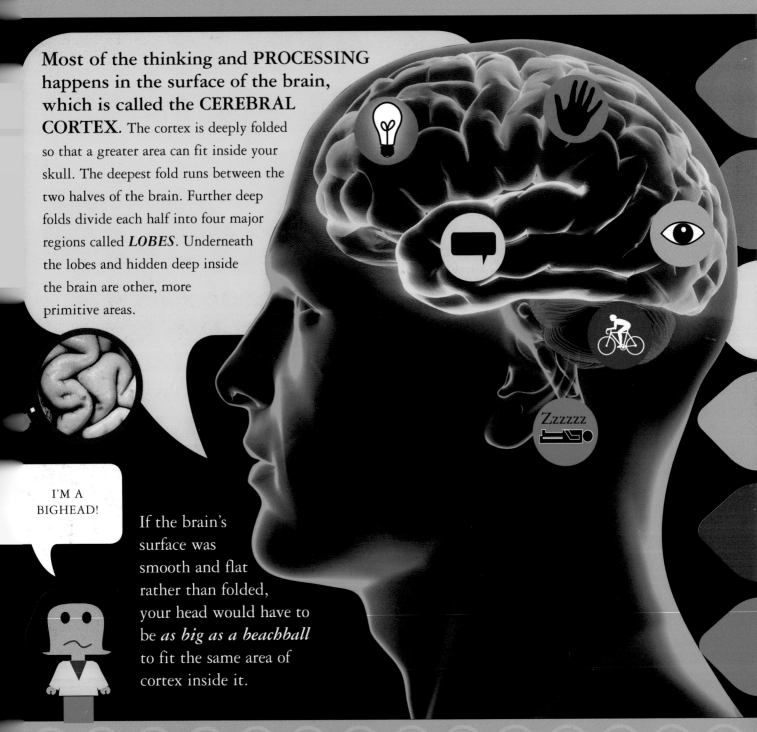

Most of the thinking and **PROCESSING** happens in the surface of the brain, which is called the **CEREBRAL CORTEX**. The cortex is deeply folded so that a greater area can fit inside your skull. The deepest fold runs between the two halves of the brain. Further deep folds divide each half into four major regions called *LOBES*. Underneath the lobes and hidden deep inside the brain are other, more primitive areas.

I'M A BIGHEAD!

If the brain's surface was smooth and flat rather than folded, your head would have to be *as big as a beachball* to fit the same area of cortex inside it.

Zzzzzz

Question: What percentage of *the brain* is water?

Two brains in one

The main part of your brain is split into two halves or **CEREBRAL HEMISPHERES**. These are a mirror image of each other, giving you (in some respects) two brains in one. This is a handy arrangement because if one side gets damaged, the other side may be able to take over (though not always). It's a bit like having two ears and two eyes – you've got a spare. The left hemisphere controls the right side of your body and sees the right side of your visual field, while the right hemisphere takes care of the left side.

FRONTAL lobe (front lobe)

Much of your thinking happens in this lobe. You use it for PLANNING, REASONING, figuring out people's thoughts, and hiding your own.

PARIETAL lobe (top lobe)

Among other jobs, this lobe processes INFORMATION coming from *senses* such as TOUCH, TASTE, AND PAIN.

TEMPORAL lobe (side lobe)

The temporal lobe plays a very important role in hearing, SPEECH, and in laying down long-term *memories*.

OCCIPITAL lobe (back lobe)

This part of the brain is where *information* from your eyes is processed so your brain can build an inner IMAGE of the world.

CEREBELLUM

Tucked under the back of the two hemispheres is a single, separate structure: the CEREBELLUM. It COORDINATES your muscles so they all work in perfect time, like a conductor keeping the musicians in an orchestra on time.

BRAIN stem

Nerves from your body join the brain at its base in a structure called the BRAIN STEM. The brain stem controls *vital functions* that keep you alive, such as HEARTBEAT and BREATHING.

BRAIN SIZE

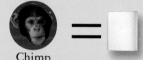

Human, Chimp, Monkey, Rat

It's not the size of a brain that makes it clever – it's the area of the cortex. Human brains are so big and folded they have **four times** as much **cortical area** as chimpanzees, our closest relatives. If the cortex of your brain was unfolded and laid out flat, it would be about the same area as four pages of this book.

LIMBIC SYSTEM

Deep inside the brain is a complicated set of structures that look very different from the folded cortex. Called the "limbic system", these parts of the brain generate powerful, instinctive emotions like fear and excitement. The human limbic system is much like that of other animals, and some scientists see it as a very ancient part of the brain where primitive "animal urges" come from.

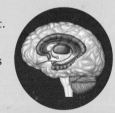

BLOOD SUPPLY

The brain is a *very* hungry organ. It takes up only 2% of your weight but it uses **20% OF YOUR ENERGY**. (Don't panic – it runs on only 20 watts, about the same as a low-energy lamp.) To keep the brain fuelled with the sugar and oxygen it needs, the heart pumps 20% of the body's blood supply to it.

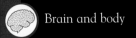

Brain *cells*

To find out what your brain is really made of, we need to zoom in with a microscope until we can see individual cells. The cells in the brain are called nerve cells or NEURONS. They are connected to each other in a complicated maze and make your brain work somewhat like a computer.

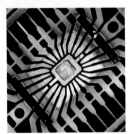

A computer chip is made up of a few million transistors, each with three or four connections.

PROCESSING POWER

The human brain has 100 billion neurons, each with up to 10,000 connections. That gives the human brain a staggering 500,000 times as many connections as the most advanced computer chip. On top of that, the human brain can effortlessly do what computer scientists call "massively parallel processing", which is like running thousands of computers together to work on the same task.

What is more powerful...

Supercomputer

The brain can *rewire* itself, **pruning** unused connections

NEURONS

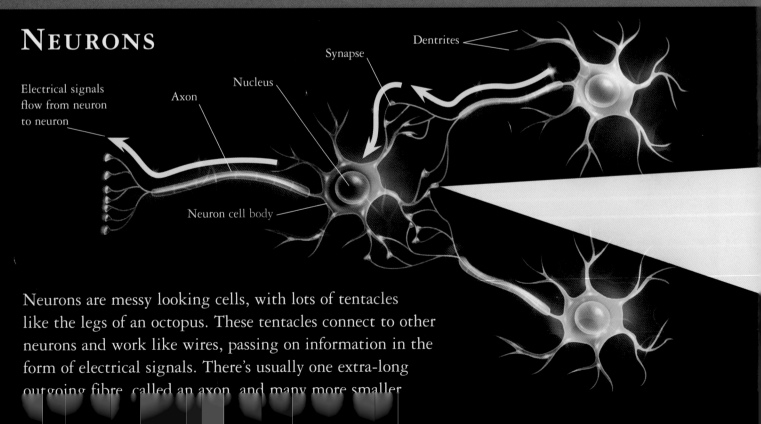

Electrical signals flow from neuron to neuron

Axon

Nucleus

Synapse

Dentrites

Neuron cell body

Neurons are messy looking cells, with lots of tentacles like the legs of an octopus. These tentacles connect to other neurons and work like wires, passing on information in the form of electrical signals. There's usually one extra-long outgoing fibre, called an axon, and many more smaller

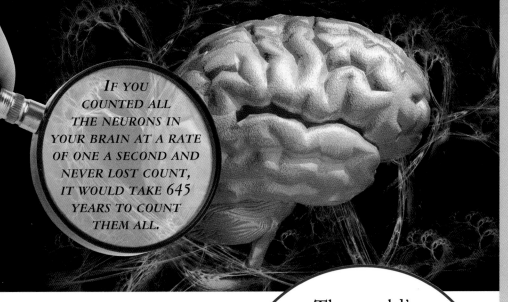

IF YOU COUNTED ALL THE NEURONS IN YOUR BRAIN AT A RATE OF ONE A SECOND AND NEVER LOST COUNT, IT WOULD TAKE 645 YEARS TO COUNT THEM ALL.

It's all grey and white

If you cut a slice through a dead brain, you'd see that the outer part looks a yellowy grey, while the inner area is paler. These two areas are known as grey and white matter. White matter is made up of axons bundled together like electric cables. These run across the brain connecting different areas together. Grey matter consists of neuron cell bodies and billions of dendrites, and this is where most of the heavy computation takes place.

supercomputer or mouse?

The world's **top** *supercomputer* is only about as powerful as HALF A MOUSE BRAIN yet it takes up more than *a million times* as much space.

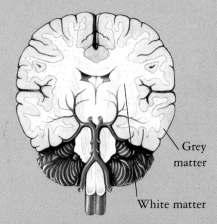

Grey matter

White matter

and building new ones as it LEARNS and *adapts*.

Electricity in the body

Neurons carry electrical signals, but they work in a different way from electric wires. When a neuron is resting, it pumps positively charged sodium atoms (from sodium chloride – ordinary salt) to the outside of the cell, where they build up like water behind a dam. When an electrical signal arrives, the floodgates open and the charged atoms rush back inside the cell, causing an electrical charge to shoot along the axon at speeds of up to 430 km/h (370 mph).

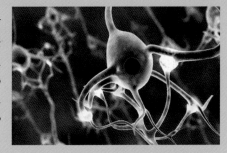

Neurotransmitters

SYNAPSE

Neurons connect to each other at junctions called **SYNAPSES**. The electrical signal can't flow across the synapse because there's a tiny gap. Instead, the synapse releases special chemicals, called NEUROTRANSMITTERS, that travel across the gap and trigger an electrical impulse in the next neuron.

Neurons and synapses come in many different shapes, sizes, and varieties, making the brain all the more complicated and its computing powers even greater.

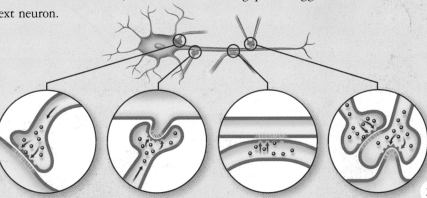

Mapping the *mind*

For centuries, people have been trying to find out what the different parts of the brain are for. Does each bit *specialize* in a particular task, like a blade on a Swiss Army knife, or do the parts work together, their cells TEAMING UP in ever-changing networks? It's a puzzle that science has yet to solve.

A BUMP ON THE HEAD

A German doctor named Franz Joseph Gall announced in the 1790s that he could tell a person's character by feeling their skull for bumps. Gall's theory was that the parts of the brain we use most grow larger, like muscles, making the head bulge in certain places. His system was called PHRENOLOGY and it became all the rage, though there wasn't a shred of evidence that it worked. He divided the brain into "organs", which he gave long names such as "amativeness" (jargon for being loving). Gall reckoned he could say whether a person was a loving parent, a devout Christian, or a calculating murderer just by feeling their head.

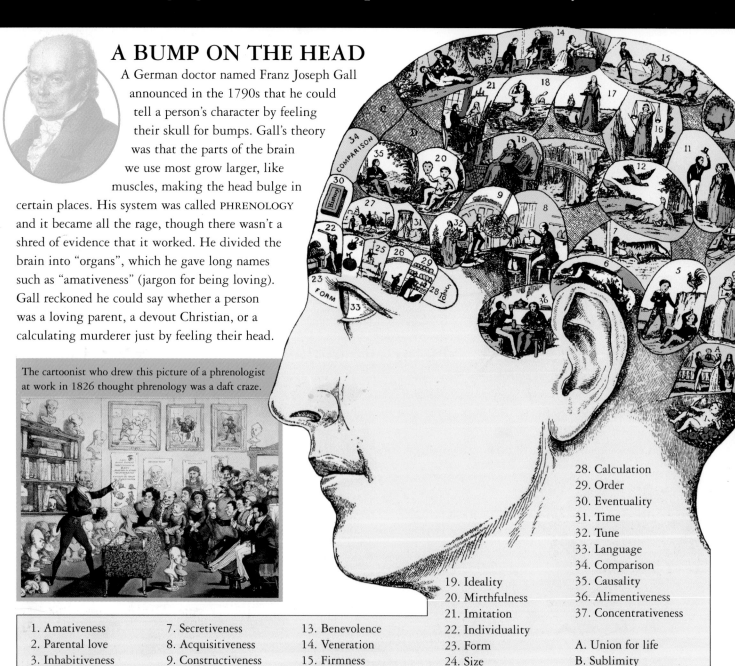

The cartoonist who drew this picture of a phrenologist at work in 1826 thought phrenology was a daft craze.

1. Amativeness	7. Secretiveness	13. Benevolence	19. Ideality	28. Calculation
2. Parental love	8. Acquisitiveness	14. Veneration	20. Mirthfulness	29. Order
3. Inhabitiveness	9. Constructiveness	15. Firmness	21. Imitation	30. Eventuality
4. Friendship	10. Self-esteem	16. Conscientiousness	22. Individuality	31. Time
5. Combativeness	11. Approbativeness	17. Hope	23. Form	32. Tune
6. Destructiveness	12. Cautiousness	18. Spirituality	24. Size	33. Language
			25. Weight	34. Comparison
			26. Colour	35. Causality
			27. Locality	36. Alimentiveness
				37. Concentrativeness
				A. Union for life
				B. Sublimity
				C. Human nature
				D. Agreeableness
				E. Vitativeness

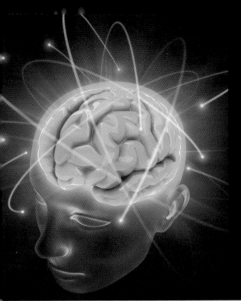

"A PIECE OF THOROUGH QUACKERY FROM BEGINNING TO END."

Scottish anatomist John Gordon's opinion of phrenology, printed in the Edinburgh Review, 1815

MODERN MAPS

When brain scanners were invented in the 1970s, they began to reveal that different parts of the brain do indeed have different functions, so there was a grain of truth in phrenology after all. Modern scanners used by brain scientists detect where brain cells are using up energy most quickly and show these areas of activity as coloured highlights on an image. Although scanning has shown that some actions, such as speaking, are controlled by specific areas, it has also revealed the brain to be highly interconnected, with memory, perception, pain, and many other functions involving huge areas of the brain firing in complex circuits.

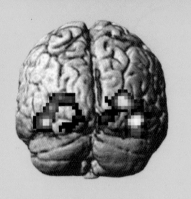

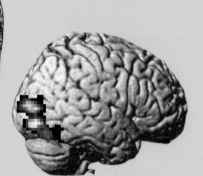

The brain scans above show parts of the back of the brain lighting up as a person spots a happy face.

Mapping the mind

THE MAN INSIDE YOUR HEAD

A large part of the brain's surface forms a kind of map of the body. American brain scientist Wilder Penfield (1891–1976) made this discovery in the 1950s. While treating patients with epilepsy, he used an electric needle to test a section of their brain's surface called the sensory cortex (which monitors sensations). As Penfield moved the needle around, the patients felt things in different bits of their body. When Penfield drew his findings onto a plan, he discovered the brain has much more space for some body parts, such as the lips and tongue.

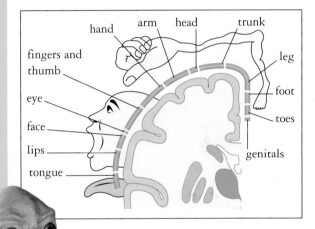

The sensitive bits

This hideous creature is what you look like according to your own sensory cortex – that part of your brain that receives touch information. It is a 3-D version of the mental body map discovered by Penfield. The sensory cortex doesn't have much space for the trunk and arms because it doesn't care much about them. It is more interested in touch information from sensitive parts, such as the fingers and lips, so they are huge in its "mind's eye".

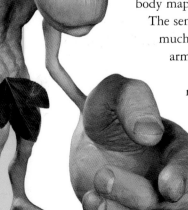

23

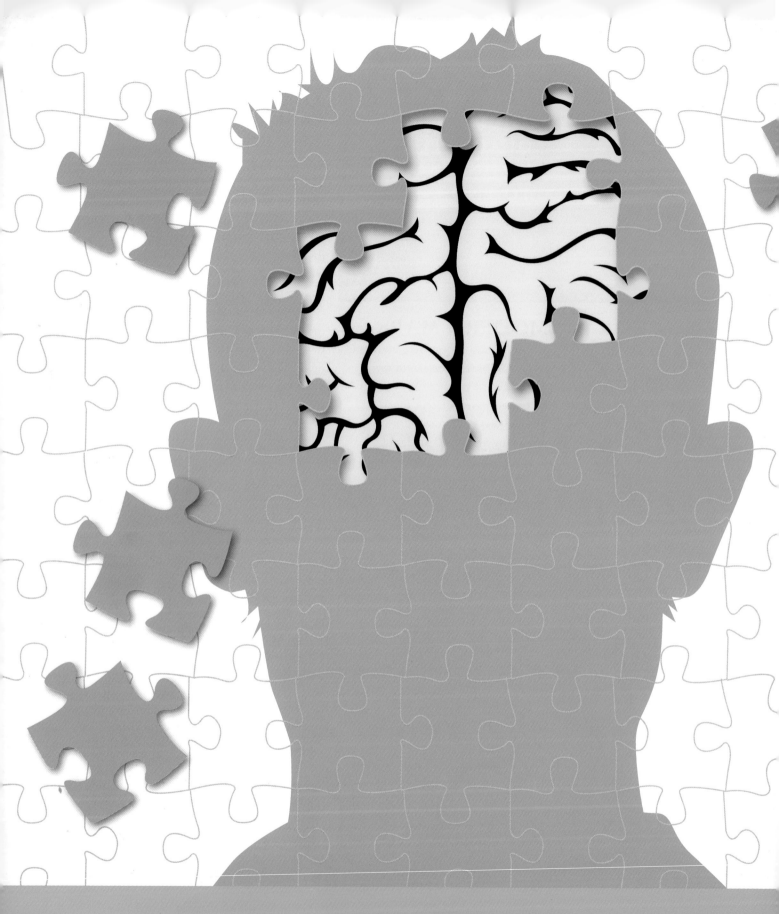

 BRAIN *and body*

...consists of an *intricate maze* of electrical circuits, but those circuits aren't confined to your head. Your brain is WIRED INTO EVERY PART of your body through a vast network of neurons that reaches down your spine and extends out to the tip of *every finger and toe*. These neurons monitor the world around you and send the data back to the brain to give you *senses*. And they direct your body's every action, governing your movements and coordinating the daily cycle of activity and sleep.

Nerve

The brain doesn't work alone – it is part of an extensive *network* of neurons called the nervous system, which runs throughout the body, directing and coordinating every activity. The nervous system performs two jobs: it takes information in through the SENSES and, after the *brain* has processed the information, it sends out new signals telling the body how to **react**.

The nervous system's control centre is called the **CENTRAL NERVOUS SYSTEM** and consists of both the brain and the spinal cord – a thick bundle of nerves that runs down the spine. From the spinal cord, nerves reach out to every part of the body, forming the **PERIPHERAL NERVOUS SYSTEM**.

Much of the peripheral nervous system is under your **control**, but some of it is **involuntary**. When you're scared, the involuntary branch of your nervous system sends the message to your heart to speed up. Vital functions like your heartbeat and breathing are controlled by the brain stem – the part of the brain joined to the spinal cord. The brain stem can keep your body *alive* even if the rest of the brain is dead.

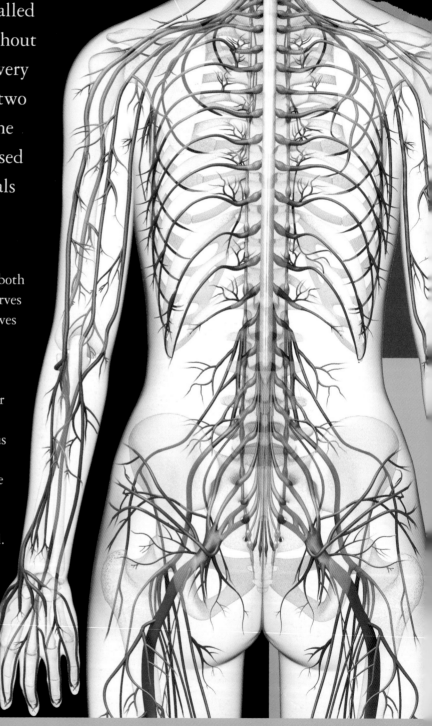

I WISH I COULD SEE WHERE I'M GOING!

ALMOST BRAINLESS
An American chicken called Mike survived for 18 months after a botched attempt to decapitate him left part of his brain stem behind.

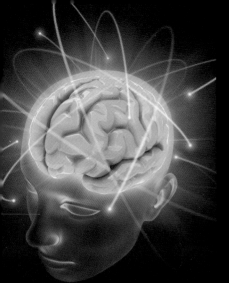

"A PIECE OF THOROUGH QUACKERY FROM BEGINNING TO END."

Scottish anatomist John Gordon's opinion of phrenology, printed in the Edinburgh Review, 1815

THE MAN INSIDE YOUR HEAD

Mapping the mind

A large part of the brain's surface forms a kind of map of the body. American brain scientist Wilder Penfield (1891–1976) made this discovery in the 1950s. While treating patients with epilepsy, he used an electric needle to test a section of their brain's surface called the sensory cortex (which monitors sensations). As Penfield moved the needle around, the patients felt things in different bits of their body. When Penfield drew his findings onto a plan, he discovered the brain has much more space for some body parts, such as the lips and tongue.

MODERN MAPS

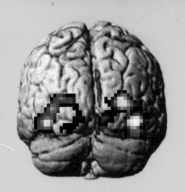

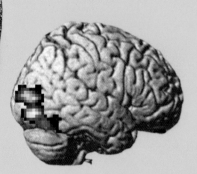

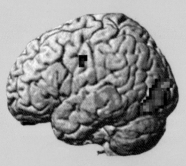

The brain scans above show parts of the back of the brain lighting up as a person spots a happy face.

When brain scanners were invented in the 1970s, they began to reveal that different parts of the brain do indeed have different functions, so there was a grain of truth in phrenology after all. Modern scanners used by brain scientists detect where brain cells are using up energy most quickly and show these areas of activity as coloured highlights on an image. Although scanning has shown that some actions, such as speaking, are controlled by specific areas, it has also revealed the brain to be highly interconnected, with memory, perception, pain, and many other functions involving huge areas of the brain firing in complex circuits.

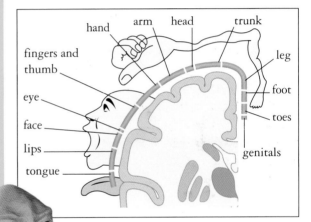

The sensitive bits

This hideous creature is what you look like according to your own sensory cortex – that part of your brain that receives touch information. It is a 3-D version of the mental body map discovered by Penfield. The sensory cortex doesn't have much space for the trunk and arms because it doesn't care much about them. It is more interested in touch information from sensitive parts, such as the fingers and lips, so they are huge in its "mind's eye".

23

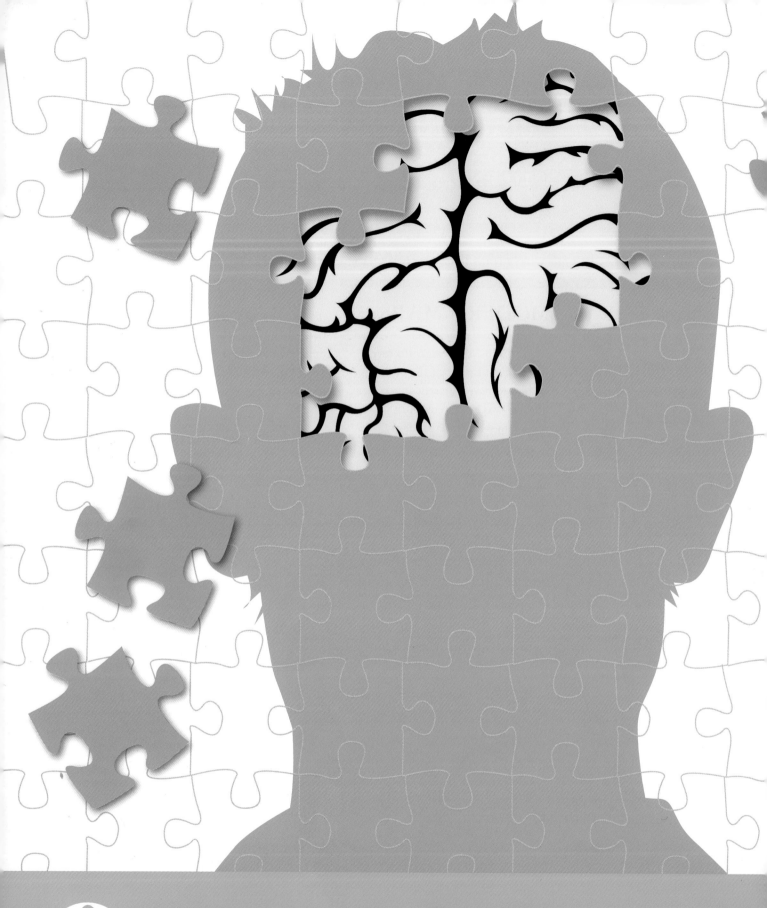

 BRAIN *and body*

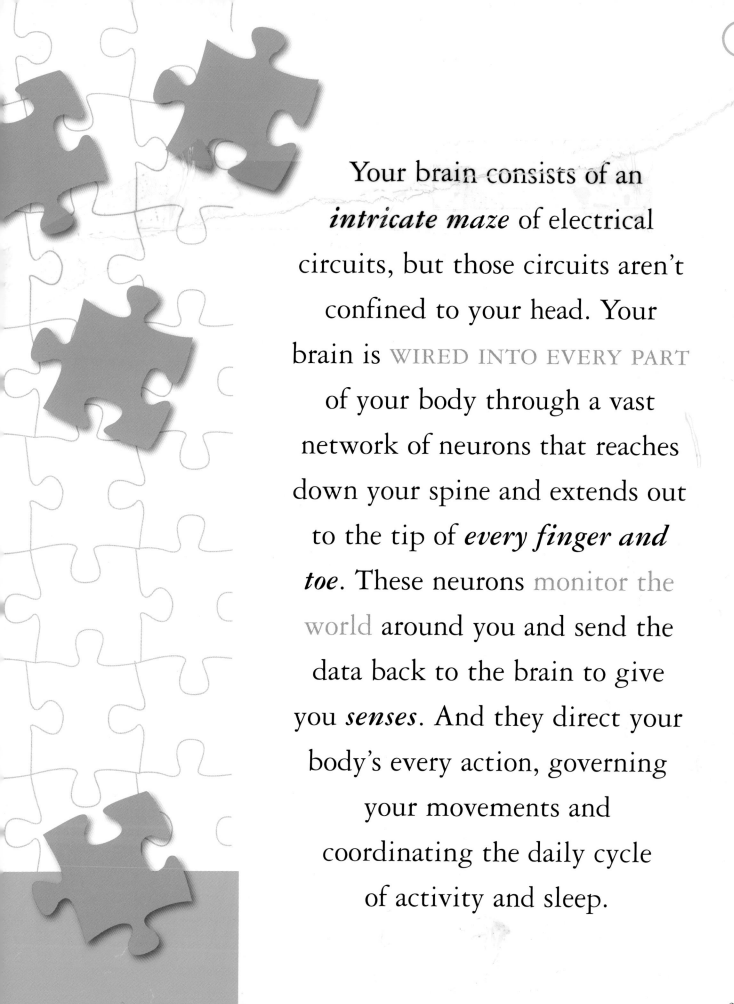

Your brain consists of an *intricate maze* of electrical circuits, but those circuits aren't confined to your head. Your brain is WIRED INTO EVERY PART of your body through a vast network of neurons that reaches down your spine and extends out to the tip of *every finger and toe*. These neurons monitor the world around you and send the data back to the brain to give you *senses*. And they direct your body's every action, governing your movements and coordinating the daily cycle of activity and sleep.

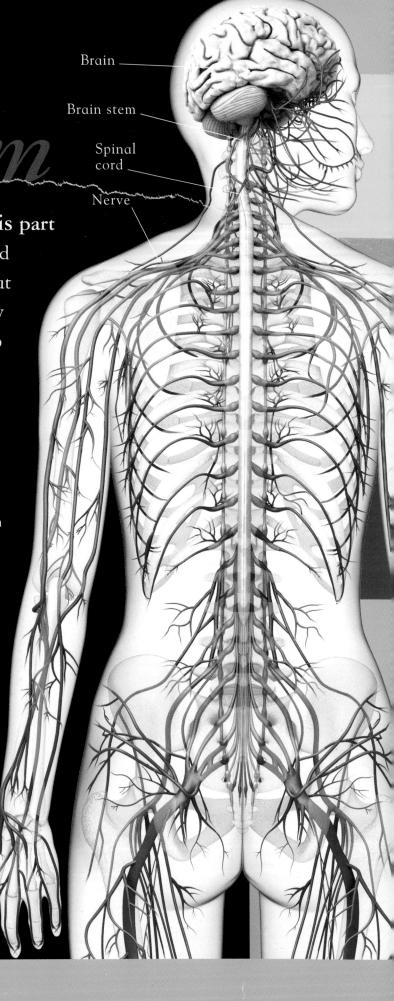

Brain

Brain stem

Spinal cord

Nerve

Nervous *system*

The brain doesn't work alone – it is part of an extensive *network* of neurons called the nervous system, which runs throughout the body, directing and coordinating every activity. The nervous system performs two jobs: it takes information in through the SENSES and, after the *brain* has processed the information, it sends out new signals telling the body how to **react**.

The nervous system's control centre is called the **CENTRAL NERVOUS SYSTEM** and consists of both the brain and the spinal cord – a thick bundle of nerves that runs down the spine. From the spinal cord, nerves reach out to every part of the body, forming the **PERIPHERAL NERVOUS SYSTEM**.

Much of the peripheral nervous system is under your **control**, but some of it is **involuntary**. When you're scared, the involuntary branch of your nervous system sends the message to your heart to speed up. Vital functions like your heartbeat and breathing are controlled by the brain stem – the part of the brain joined to the spinal cord. The brain stem can keep your body *alive* even if the rest of the brain is dead.

I WISH I COULD SEE WHERE I'M GOING!

ALMOST BRAINLESS
An American chicken called Mike survived for 18 months after a botched attempt to decapitate him left part of his brain stem behind.

THE SENSES

Vision

When the neurons in our eyes are struck by light rays, they send signals to the brain, creating the sense of vision. Vision is our most important sense, with a huge area of the brain dedicated to processing what we see.

Hearing

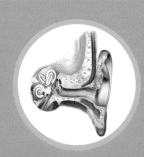

Our ears detect air vibrations that we call sound. Sound waves are funnelled into the ear and are transmitted across the middle ear by a tiny drum and series of levers. These vibrations set off nerve cells in the inner ear that send signals to the brain.

Smell

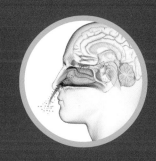

The sense of smell enables you to detect odour molecules. The lining of the nose and passages behind it are full of sensors that can detect between 4000 and 10,000 different smells. Your brain puts the signals together to tell you what the smelly object is.

Taste

The tongue can detect only five tastes: sweet, sour, salty, bitter, and savoury. Combining these with smell signals helps the brain tell the difference between cherries, cheese, and toast.

Touch

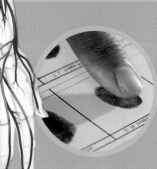

The skin is full of sensors that respond to different touch sensations, such as firm pressure, stroking, light touch, and vibration. Your sense of touch is so good that you can work out what objects are with your eyes closed.

SPECIAL SENSES

Besides the five main senses, humans have a number of other senses that play an important role in how our bodies work and how we interact with the environment around us. Many of them work without us even being aware of them.

GRAVITY affects tiny sensors in your ears called otoliths, which tell your brain which way is up and which is down, helping you balance.

MOTION is also picked up by sensors in your ears. You can confuse these sensors by spinning around very fast until you feel dizzy.

POSTURE is detected in your muscles and joints by stretch receptors that tell your brain the position and movement of the bits of your body.

HEAT sensors respond to a rise in temperature, whether it's caused by the Sun's rays, a hot cup of coffee, or a fever brought on by an illness.

COLD receptors react to low temperatures, causing goosebumps on your skin as body hairs rise to try and keep you warm.

PAIN is a special sense that warns you about things that might cause injury or affect your health. Itching and tickling are related to pain.

DIRECTION is a sense humans probably don't have, but many animals do because they can tune into Earth's magnetic field to find their way.

CALLS OF NATURE involve stretch sensors in organs like your bladder and bowels that tell you when they're full and ready to let go.

Vision

The light-sensitive retina inside the eye is wired to the back of the brain via a cable called the optic nerve.

The sense of vision is the *main* way in which your brain takes in INFORMATION about the world. Your eyes are extensions of your brain, *small periscopes* that poke through holes in your skull to let **light** onto the brain's surface. Lining the back of each eye are *125 million* light-sensing neurons forming a layer called a RETINA.

Visual cortex — Optic nerve — Retina — Eye

LIVING CAMERAS

An eye works much like a camera, but its lenses are made of clear jelly or fluid rather than glass. Like a camera, it uses curved lenses to focus captured light rays onto a light-sensitive film (the retina) on its back surface, forming an upside-down image. Cameras adjust their focus by moving the lens in and out, but eyes use muscles to stretch an adjustable lens.

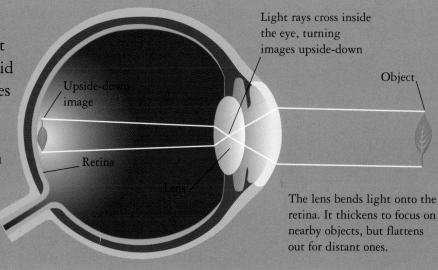

Light rays cross inside the eye, turning images upside-down

Upside-down image

Retina

Lens

Object

The lens bends light onto the retina. It thickens to focus on nearby objects, but flattens out for distant ones.

See *inside* your eyes!

This trick allows you to see your own retina. You need a dim torch with the bulb exposed and a piece of black paper. In a very dark room, hold the paper so it fills your field of vision. Hold the torch 1 cm (0.5 in) in front of and below your eyes (taking care not to poke an eye) and stare at the paper. A tree-like shape will appear – the shadow of your retina's blood vessels.

Rods and cones

The photoreceptors on the surface of the retina come in two main types: rods and cones. These have different strengths and weaknesses. Cones can see colour and fine details, but they need bright light to work. Rods work in very dim light, but they see in black-and-white and pick up less detail. When you try to see in the dark, only your rods are working and so the world becomes colourless. Switch on a light and your cones switch on too, flooding the image in your mind with colour and detail.

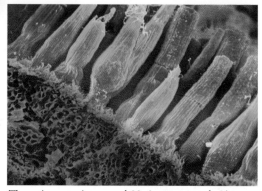

The retina contains around 20 times more rods (shown in artificially coloured blue) than cones (blue-green).

The eye's spotlight

When you look directly at something, such as this word, you see it much more clearly and sharply than things elsewhere in your field of vision (your peripheral vision). This is because you use a special part of the retina – the fovea – to see objects in the middle of your field of vision. The fovea is packed with cones and has few rods, giving better colour and detail than any other part of the eye.

COLOUR *on the edge*

Your peripheral vision is lousy at seeing colour. Ask a friend to slowly move a coloured pencil from behind you into your peripheral vision while you stare straight ahead. Tell them to stop moving it as soon as you see it. What colour is it? It will look black at first, but move it a little further and its colour will appear.

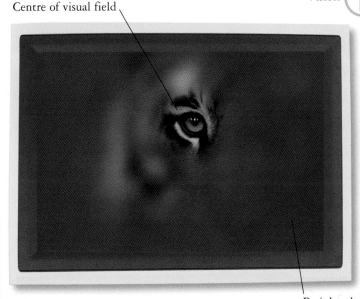

Centre of visual field

Peripheral vision

The fovea isn't very good in the dark. To see faint stars at night, look away from them slightly so you see them with your peripheral vision, where there are more rods.

THE VISUAL PATHWAY

The light your eyes captures is converted into electrical signals that pass to the back of the brain to be processed in the visual cortex. The rods and cones that pick up light from the left side of the visual field are wired into the right half of the brain, and vice versa. People with brain damage to one half of the brain may not see the whole visual field – so may eat all the food on the left of the plate, but not see any on the right.

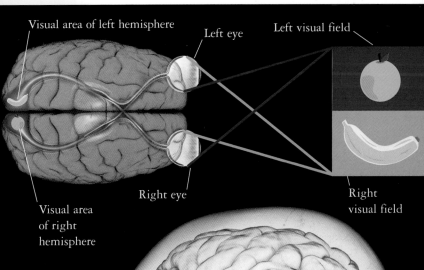

Visual area of left hemisphere

Left eye

Left visual field

Visual area of right hemisphere

Right eye

Right visual field

EYES IN THE BACK OF THE HEAD

During World War II, aptly named British doctor Henry Head discovered that soldiers with shrapnel injuries in the back of the brain had strange blind spots in their field of vision. Henry Head had discovered the visual cortex – the part of the brain that processes images. As signals from the eyes pass through the visual cortex, different strips of cortex detect different bits of information, such as edges, colours, motion, angles, and simple shapes. Bit by bit, the image is broken down into a set of clues that are forwarded to other parts of the brain so that objects can be recognized.

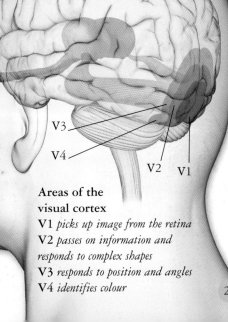

V3
V4
V2 V1

Areas of the visual cortex
V1 *picks up image from the retina*
V2 *passes on information and responds to complex shapes*
V3 *responds to position and angles*
V4 *identifies colour*

29

PERCEPTION

The image of the world that we see in our mind's eye is not simply a snapshot like a photograph. The complex patterns of light and shade captured by our eyes are processed by the brain to give the images *meaning*. Perception involves not just vision but also memory, experience, expectations, and even imagination.

WHAT ARE *THESE*..?

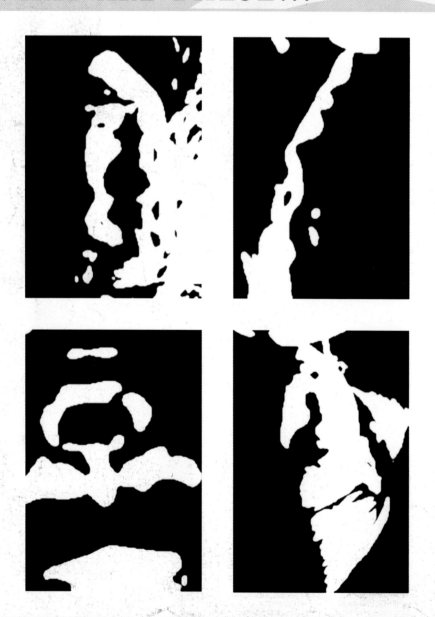

If you're stuck, turn the page upside down. You can *see* the images whichever way up they are, but you don't *recognize* them until they're the right way up. Human brains are programmed to recognize faces – provided they are upright – from the sketchiest of details. We can even perceive the sex, race, age, and mood of the people in the images from nothing more than a few white squiggles. This skill depends on a part of the brain's temporal (side) lobe called the fusiform face area. The visual cortex sends signals here so we can quickly identify people and assess their mood. Damage to the fusiform face area causes a rare condition called prosopagnosia in which a sufferer can't even recognize their own family.

A human face on Mars..? ... The "face" revealed.

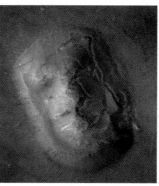

Face on Mars

Our brains are *so* good at spotting **faces** that we can see some that aren't even there. In 1976, the Viking spacecraft took a photograph of what appeared to be a huge sculpture of a human face on Mars. This led to outlandish theories about *alien visitors* or ancient Martian civilizations. Around 22 years later, the Mars Orbiter sent back a new image of the face showing it was just a TRICK of the light.

Mona Lisa by Leonardo da Vinci

The *Mona Lisa*'s secret?

Is the *Mona Lisa* smiling? This enigma has baffled people for years, but one scientist thinks she may have solved the riddle. According to Professor Margaret Livingstone of Harvard University, the *smile* only appears when you look away from her face. Livingstone says that when we look away, we see the face with our peripheral vision, picking up shadows and patterns that suggest she's smiling. But when we look *directly* at her mouth, we use our fovea, the sharpest point of vision, which picks up finer details (such as the flat mouth) that suggest she isn't smiling.

LOOK at this painting of the countryside in summer and, before you read on, think of four or five adjectives that describe it.

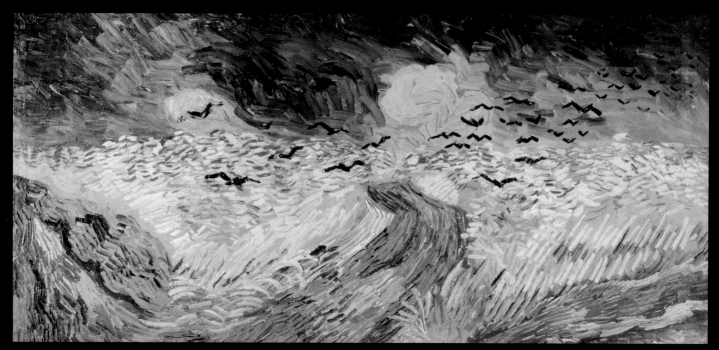

Wheatfield with Crows by Vincent van Gogh, 1890

You might have thought of words like sunny, tranquil, or natural. Now take another look, bearing in mind that the artist van Gogh painted this scene just before he killed himself as a result of depression. Does the scene now appear gloomy, dark, or disturbing? What we see depends on our expectations. Knowing that van Gogh was suicidally unhappy when he painted the field gives the image an emotional meaning and focuses our attention on its DARKER elements: the stormy sky, the black crows fleeing, and the lonely emptiness of the field.

STOP! What are you *really*

An Unexpected Visitor by Ilya Repin, 1884.

SEEING WITHOUT SEEING

It takes only a fraction of a second for the brain to process an image from your eyes and make you consciously aware of what you're looking at. But this isn't always fast enough. What if a rock is hurtling towards you or a snake lunges up from the grass? In dangerous situations where rapid reactions are vital, the brain relies on a processing shortcut known as the **low road** that causes the body to react before you're conscious of what you've seen. On the way to the **visual cortex**, which creates conscious vision, signals from your eyes pass through the **thalamus**, which recognizes simple threats such as snake-like objects and sends a signal to the **amygdala**, triggering a "fight or flight" reaction.

LOOKING at?

By tracking eye movements when people view images such as the painting on the left, scientists have found out how the brain takes in a scene. We don't simply take in a snapshot in one glance, as you might think. Instead, our eyes dart about quickly and instinctively, gathering information as the FOVEA (the high-resolution part of the retina) rests briefly on one detail after another. The brain directs the eyes to parts of the scene it considers significant – especially faces – and disregards much of the rest. Why faces? To humans, faces are a vital source of information about people, their relationships, and their intentions.

Above: Eye-tracking studies record eye movements, revealing which parts of the painting viewers look at in the first few seconds.

Below: As well as focusing on faces, we follow each person's gaze to see what they are looking at (and therefore thinking about).

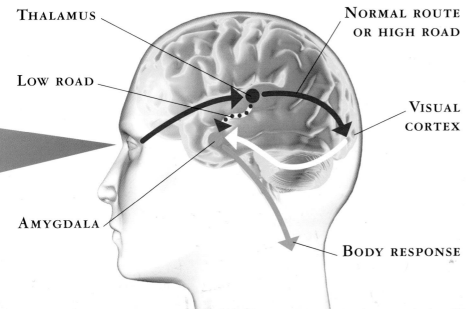

THALAMUS

LOW ROAD

AMYGDALA

NORMAL ROUTE OR HIGH ROAD

VISUAL CORTEX

BODY RESPONSE

OUT OF SIGHT

Mind the gaps

You're blind for about 90 minutes every day with your eyes open. When your eyes dart from place to place (a saccade), your brain temporarily ignores signals from the retina, otherwise your vision would be blurry. You don't notice because your brain fills in the gaps, but you can prove the blindness happens by looking alternately at your left and right eyes in a mirror. You won't be able to spot the motion – it's impossible.

Stopping time

Have you ever glanced at a clock and thought the second hand was frozen, only for it to start moving after what seems like more than a second? This is called the "stopped clock illusion" and is caused by your eyes saccading to the clock and your brain filling in the gap by "backdating" the image of the clock, making that second seem longer than a second.

Constant movement

As well as darting about, our eyes vibrate back and forth by a tiny amount up to 40 times a second. These movements, called microsaccades, are essential as the retina responds only to *changes* in light. If the image is frozen by floating a tiny viewing device on a person's eye, the image fades in seconds. The blood vessels on the retina are invisible to us because they move with the eyeball.

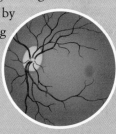

Blood vessels in the retina

SEEING IN 3D

To catch a ball, jump over a fence, or pour a cup of coffee, it helps if you can SEE in 3D. Three-dimensional vision allows us to judge DEPTH and d i s t a n c e, telling our brains *exactly* how far we need to move to pick something up or avoid collisions.

SEEING DOUBLE

Hold your finger in front of your face and close your right eye. Now close your left. Your finger appears to have moved! We have two eyes, so we see the world twice, at two different angles. The nearer an object is, the more different it looks to the right and left eye. The brain uses these differences to work out where an object is and create an awareness of 3D. 3D films use a similar idea: each scene is filmed by a pair of cameras set apart like eyes. Viewers wear special glasses so that each eye sees only what it is meant to.

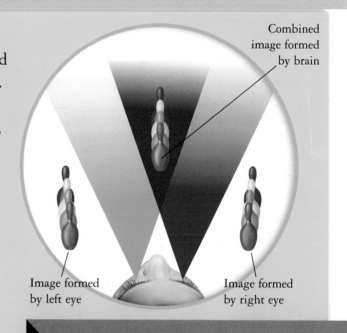

Combined image formed by brain

Image formed by left eye

Image formed by right eye

One giant leap – off the page!

You don't need special glasses to see in 3D: this stereogram allows you to see the Moon landing in 3D simply by crossing your eyes (which may take a bit of practice). First hold the pair of pictures about half an arm's length away from your eyes. Stare into the middle and cross your eyes so you see three images. They will be blurred at first, but hold your attention on the central blurry image. Slowly it will come into focus, revealing the scene in dramatic 3D.

Hidden images

Autostereograms contain hidden 3D images. Hold the page close, and relax your eyes to look through the image so it's blurred. The repeating patterns of dots seen by your right and left eyes will slide around as your eyes change their focus. Be patient, and the repeating patterns might overlap so they match, fooling your brain into thinking the image is in focus. When that happens, the hidden object will slowly appear.

3D CLUES

Stereo vision isn't the only source of 3D information our brains use. There are many other clues as well. Artists exploit these clues to give depth to scenes or to trick your brain into seeing the impossible.

1 When we see parallel lines that converge (draw together), our brains assume the lines are **receding** (going into the distance).

2 **Shadows** reveal the shape of 3D objects.

3 Details **fade with distance** – so separate leaves become a blur of green.

4 If one object is **behind** another, it must be further away...

5 ... And if there are several objects we know to be the same size (such as people) then the smaller ones must be **further away.**

Motion clues

Even with one eye closed you can judge depth by moving your head from side to side, because distant objects seem to keep still while nearby objects move more.

A spitting cobra swings its head left to right to pinpoint its prey

Distance fog

Outdoors, distant objects such as hills usually appear hazy and bluish, with less colour than nearby objects. This is because dust in the air filters out much of the light.

Computer games use fog to create distance

Depth of field

When you focus on a nearby object, things in the background are blurred. Photographers blur objects in the background to draw attention to those in front, making them stand out.

The pig appears 3D next to the blurred car

Ice see it now

It looks like a glacier has split apart, sending chunks of ice tumbling a long way down – but this clever illusion is simply a chalk drawing on the pavement. The artist has used shading, converging lines, and other tricks of perspective (angle of view) to make a two-dimensional image trick our brains into seeing a three-dimensional world that isn't there.

This amazing 3D street art was created by artist Edgar Mueller.

Illusions

In order to *make sense* of the images captured by our eyes, the brain must extract clues from the images and then interpret the clues correctly by using rules of thumb about the world. Illusions reveal what those rules of thumb are by breaking the rules and making us see *impossible or nonsensical images*.

Which is bigger?

Believe it not, the yellow lines on the left are exactly the same size, and so are the tigers on the right. So why does one look bigger? When we see straight lines that taper together, it's usually because they're getting further away. Our brains use this rule of thumb to perceive distance. We see the third tiger as farther away, so we also see it as bigger.

Which is darker?

Does square A look darker than B? They're exactly the same, as the smaller picture proves. The main rule of thumb being tricked is that objects in the shade reflect less light. Our brains compensate for this effect by telling us to perceive B as brighter than it really is. For the same reason, a snowball always looks white to us – even when we take it indoors and it actually becomes grey.

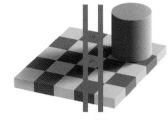

Rules of thumb our brains use:
1. Objects in shadow reflect less light.
2. Shadows usually have soft edges.

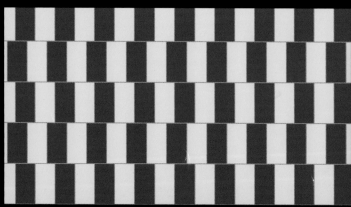

Wonky or straight? The horizontal lines are dead straight but appear to slope. This illusion works by exploiting a flaw in the way neurons in the brain's visual cortex process patterns of bright and dark shade. For complicated reasons, we see the grey lines between the squares as sloping in our peripheral vision, making the whole pattern look crooked.

Which line is longer?

Neither, they're just the same. The best explanation for this famous illusion is that the arrows trigger our brain's 3D perception system. The top line resembles a nearby edge, whereas the bottom line resembles a more distant edge, which we therefore perceive as wider since it's further away. The picture on the right shows the same red lines superimposed on walls, making the 3D effect even more powerful.

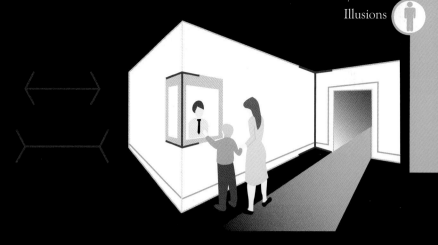

WHICH LEANING TOWER LEANS THE MOST?

Is one of these towers leaning more than the other? No, it's the same photo and they're leaning at the same angle. Why the apparent difference then? In the real world, two parallel towers would appear to *converge* (point together) if you stood at the bottom looking up, just as parallel railway lines converge as they run into the distance. But here the towers don't converge – they remain parallel. So our brains assume they must be *diverging*, and we see one as leaning further than the other.

Rule of thumb our brains make:
1. Lines that are truly parallel always appear to converge as they run into the distance.
2. Lines that run into the distance but are parallel on the retina must be diverging.

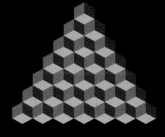

If you stare for long enough at the image on the left, it will suddenly change. The cubes will flip upside down, and the corners that stick out will suddenly point inwards. The illusion happens because there are two ways your brain can process the picture to create a 3D mental image. These two interpretations can't coexist in your brain at the same time, so your perception flips between one and the other.

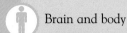

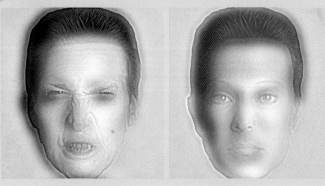

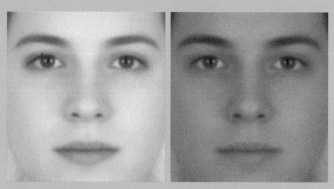

Who's angriest? Now prop the book up, walk 3 m (10 ft) away and look again. Mr Angry becomes Mr Nice and vice versa! Each image is a hybrid of two faces, one made of fine details and another made of coarser shadings. Your eyes pick up the fine details only when close. The hidden blurry face emerges when the fine details are too far away to see.

Which is male and female? We see the right face as male and the left as female, but they're actually both the same photograph of a man. The contrast between the eyes, mouth and skin has been exaggerated in the left image, producing a darker mouth and eyes. Make-up creates the same high contrast, so we see the left face as female.

Do the blue spots move about when you read these words?

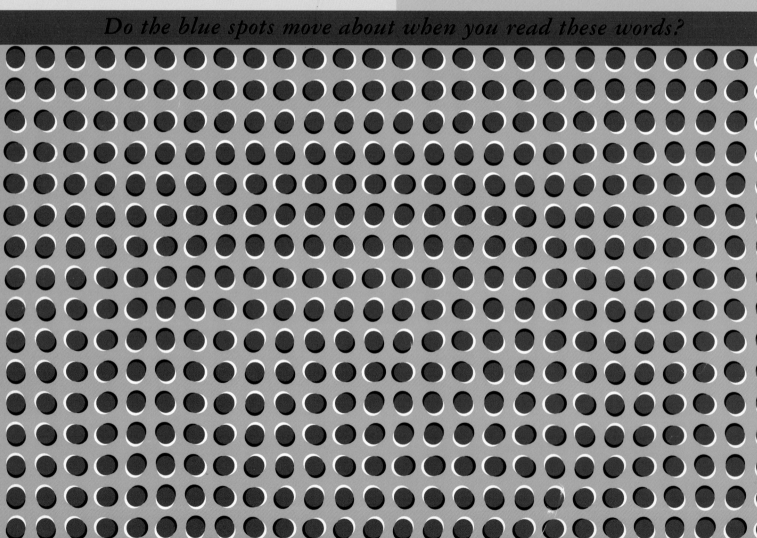

The blue dots appear to move in the corner of your eye but freeze when you look straight at one. The motion happens only in your "peripheral vision" – the parts of your field of vision that you aren't looking at directly – and only while your eyes are moving. It's caused by the pattern of repeating bright and dark bands. Bright areas are processed slightly faster by the brain's visual system. As a result, when your eyes move, the bright areas are perceived as having "got there first". The repetitive pattern also makes it hard for your brain lock on to the image and prevent the imaginary motion.

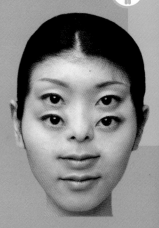

Without turning the page upside down, see if you can figure out the difference between the *Mona Lisa* here and the one on page 31. Now turn the page round. Surprised? The facial recognition area in the brain is tuned to detect upright faces only and cannot process upside-down faces, so we don't spot the flaws in this image. However, the parts of the brain that recognize eyes and mouths still work and perceive those parts of the image as normal. As a result, we don't see what a weird image this truly is until we turn it round.

Seeing double?
This illusion can make your head spin. When we look at faces our brains measure the shape of the triangle made by the eyes and mouth. This image confuses the facial recognition system by giving it two conflicting triangles. Our attention flickers from one to the other as the brain tries to lock on to the image, making us feel slightly dizzy.

ARE THE PEOPLE BELOW REAL PEOPLE OR TINY MODELS?

No it's not a tiny model, it's a real station full of real people. So why do they look so small? The photographer has used a special lens that focuses only on objects within a narrow range of distances, blurring everything else and creating what photographers call "narrow depth of field". Normally we only experience a narrow depth of field when looking at small objects close to our eyes (hold a finger up to your eyes and the background will look blurred). Our brains interpret narrow depth of field as a clue that objects are miniature, so we perceive the people as tiny models.

Body ILLUSIONS

BODY SENSES

The amazing sense that makes you aware of your body and its movements is called PROPRIOCEPTION. Special sensors inside different parts of your body tell your brain what every bit of your body is up to without you having to think about it.

Joints

Sensors in every joint tell the brain exactly where all our bones are. This helps the brain to decide which movements are safe to make. If we don't pay attention to our sensors, we may get hurt!

Muscles

Whenever we move, our muscles stretch and contract, triggering stretch sensors buried deep inside them. These send signals to the brain too.

The inner ear

Tiny gravity sensors in the inner ear help us to know which way is up or down, while tiny motion sensors inside three fluid-filled loops in the inner ear sense movement in any direction.

Cerebellum

This part of the brain is like the conductor in an orchestra. It stores learnt sequences of movement and coordinates and fine-tunes messages from elsewhere in the brain to create fluid body movements.

Balance

To help us balance, our brain has to coordinate all the visual signals from our eyes, sensory information from our ears, and proprioception signals from our muscles.

AMAZE

Hand–eye coordination

1 We tend to use our eyes to guide our hands, but you can *almost* manage with proprioception alone. Test this by drawing a square with your eyes closed. As long as you keep pen on paper it's quite easy, because your brain can rely on feedback from your hand and arm muscles to sense how it's doing.

2 Now draw a house with your eyes closed. As soon as you take your hand off the page to add details, you'll find you can't put them exactly where they need to go. It's hard to put your hands precisely where they need to be unless you have visual feedback from your eyes.

3 Now try drawing the same house in a mirror. (Don't cheat – look into the mirror the whole time.) This is surprisingly difficult because the signals your brain gets from your eyes *conflict* with those from your hand, leaving your brain confused about what to do. The secret to drawing in a mirror? Close your eyes. You'll do much better!

Your external senses of touch and vision work together with a special internal *body sense* to keep your brain aware of where every bit of your body is and how it's moving. The TRICKS on this page not only show how your internal body sense works but show you *how to fool it too*!

YOUR FRIENDS WITH THESE MIND-BENDING TRICKS!

Cross your fingers

The Aristotle illusion is one of the oldest known body illusions. Cross your fingers, then touch your nose with both fingers at the same time. Does it feel like you have two noses? Try the same trick with a marble or a pea.

Your brain receives sensory signals from the outside edges of both fingers. Because they don't usually rub against each other, your brain concludes that you must be touching two objects.

Hopping mad

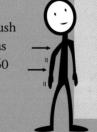

Ask your friend to close his eyes. Tap him quickly four times on the wrist, four times on the elbow, and four times at the top of his arm. Does it feel like a small rabbit is hopping up his arm?

Scientists aren't sure why we feel taps *all* along the arm, instead of in just three places, but it is thought that what the brain *expects* to happen overrides what it feels is taking place.

Hard to resist

❶ Ask a friend to stretch out his arm. Then ask him to resist as you press down on his wrist with two fingers. He should find it easy to resist the pressure.

❷ Now ask your friend to put one foot on a low pile of books or a step and repeat the test.

❸ This time, your friend won't be able to resist the pressure and you'll find it easy to force his arm down.

Pinocchio nose

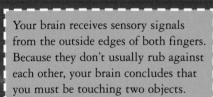

❶ Blindfold yourself and then stand behind a friend.

❷ At the same time, and with identical movements, stroke your own nose with one hand and your friend's nose with your other hand for a couple of minutes. Does your nose seem longer all of a sudden?

Your brain receives identical sensory signals from both hands and is confused into thinking you are only touching one nose. Because of a lack of visual clues and since one arm is outstretched, it concludes your nose has grown.

Levitating arm

❶ Stand straight against a wall and push your arm against it as hard as you can for 60 seconds – the harder you push, the better the final effect!

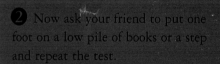

❷ Now move away from the wall. Does your arm rise up on its own?

You are tensing your arm muscles as you push against the wall. The muscles and brain adapt to this constant tension, so that when you stop, your muscles remain slightly tense and your arm rises. And if you *expect* your arm to rise, it will rise all the more.

When your friend raises one foot, his brain thinks that the spine is in a vulnerable position. In order to protect the spine from damage, the brain "turns off" the messages to the arm muscles that are making it resist, and the arm lowers.

PAIN in the BRAIN

Nothing grabs your attention quite like a sudden pain. And that's exactly what it's supposed to do. Pain is a warning sign that something is wrong with your body and that you need to do something about it before you do any further damage. Ongoing pain is a reminder not to overdo things while the injury heals.

In each *square centimetre* of skin there are **200** *pain sensors*

WHERE'S THE PAIN COMING FROM?

Our skin, muscles, and internal organs are full of sensors that respond to things such as pressure, heat, and chemicals. If any of these start to damage the body, they trigger pain sensors, which send electrical signals up the spinal cord and to a part of the brain called the thalamus. The thalamus directs the signals to other parts of the brain that figure out where the pain is coming from, what it means, and how unpleasant it should feel. The brain sends messages back to the spinal cord telling your body how to react.

3 FEEL

The brain receives the signal and interprets what kind of pain it is, how strong it is, and how much damage may have been done. Armed with this knowledge, the brain then decides what to do next.

2 REACT

The spinal cord reacts almost instantly, before the pain signal reaches the brain. It sends a new signal to your leg muscles to lift your foot off the pin.

1 DETECT

If you step on a pin, pain sensors in your skin immediately send a message about the injury to your brain. Touch sensors also send signals about what's causing the pain.

Pain is a special sense that makes an alarm ring inside your brain

Natural born painkillers

One of the brain's responses to pain is to send messages to nerve cells near the injury that contain substances called endorphins. These are released into the synapses and are taken up by the neurons that are transmitting the pain signal. Endorphins block the signal and prevent it from travelling to the brain. Endorphins have a similar chemical structure to morphine, which is used as a painkiller in hospitals. Morphine is one of several natural painkillers produced in the seed heads of the opium poppy.

Pain under strain

Acute stress can have an amazing effect on pain. Soldiers injured in battle can fight on despite the pain because their bodies are pumping out a powerful combination of stress chemicals, including adrenaline and cortisol, which trigger the release of endorphins. People have even been hit by bullets and not felt a thing. The effect doesn't last, but it is often long enough for a person to reach safety.

No pain, no gain

Psychology plays an important part in how we respond to pain. Positive thinking can have as much effect as powerful painkiller drugs. Athletes can train themselves to endure pain that would have lesser mortals in bed for a week. This ability to put "mind over matter" and block out pain is what enables people to walk over hot coals or lie on a bed of nails. By "psyching themselves up" they can reduce the amount of pain they actually feel.

Sugaring the pill

Doctors have found that giving harmless sugar pills or saltwater injections to people in pain can have the same effect as giving them real painkillers. This is known as the "placebo effect". The patient's belief that they have been given a real medicine is so strong that the pain really goes away. Brain scans even show that placebos dampen down the parts of the brain that become active during pain in just the same way as real painkillers.

Rub it better

Not all pain signals go directly to the brain. Weaker signals may be filtered out by special "gatekeeper" nerve cells in the spinal cord. Gatekeeper cells are also affected by nerve fibres that transmit touch sensations. If you sprain your ankle, it's instinctive to rub the injury. Rubbing activates touch sensors, whose signals swamp the gatekeeper cells and reduce the number of pain signals they can send to the brain. That's why rubbing the injury really does make it feel better.

PAINFUL FACTS

• Chilli contains a substance called capsaicin that causes a burning pain. Some people think the endorphins this pain releases are responsible for the pleasurable sensation caused by eating spicy food.

• Swearing really can help reduce the pain you feel when you hurt yourself. Scientists think that anger triggers the stress response, which releases chemicals that help lessen the pain. Just remember not to do it in front of Grandma...

#@%&
#£!

• A faulty gene prevents some people from feeling any pain at all. It might sound great but feeling no pain can be lethally dangerous. Pain is good for you!

FAQ

Where is the body clock?

The main body clock is near the base of the brain, next to the nerves that carry signals into the brain from the eyes. It consists of two clusters of brain cells called the suprachiasmatic nuclei (SCN). Special genes in these brain cells switch themselves on and off like clockwork, keeping time. The SCN controls wakefulness by triggering the release of hormones such as melatonin, which make us feel sleepy or alert.

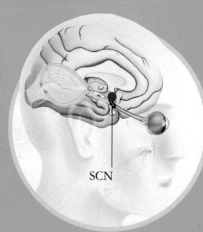

SCN

Are you an owl or a lark?

The human body clock works on a 24-hour cycle, but the length of the cycle can vary from person to person, perhaps largely for genetic reasons. People with a clock shorter than 24 hours find it easier getting up early in the morning and are known as larks. People with a longer body clock tend to stay up late at night and are called owls.

DEEP INSIDE the human brain is a living clock that acts as your body's timekeeper, telling you when to wake, sleep, rest, and play. Understanding your body clock can help you get the most out of each day.

08:30 a.m. Bowel movement most likely.

08:00–11:00 Heart attacks are most likely in the morning because the blood is sticky, blood vessels are stiffer, and blood pressure rises steeply after waking.

11:00 We are now fully alert and active, except for teenagers, who have a late-running body clock and are not fully alert until the afternoon. This late clock makes it hard for teenagers to get up early.

12:00 Around lunch, wakefulness and body temperature dip naturally, whether or not we've had a meal. "Microsleeps", where people accidentally nod off for a few seconds, can happen. In some countries, people take a siesta in the post-lunch dip.

14:00 This is the time of day when car crashes are most likely. Many motorway crashes are probably caused by drivers having microsleeps at the wheel.

16:00 Alertness and body temperature rise again. Reaction times are fastest around this time, making it the best part of the day for sporting performance.

18:00 Although the working day is over, the body clock is still in prime time, keeping us active and alert. A good time for socializing.

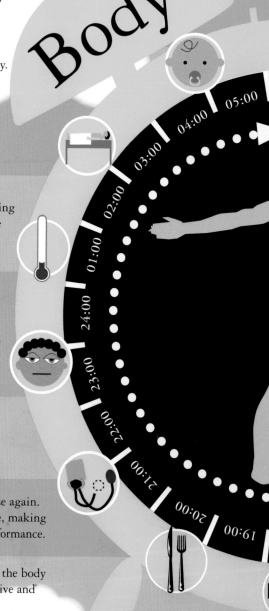

Body

The *deadliest hours* of the

Without looking at a watch or a clock, try and guess the time now. Were you close? Most people can guess the time to within TEN MINUTES without looking, thanks to their inner sense of time.

clock

19:00 Fading daylight is detected by our eyes and brain, which then tell the body that night is drawing in and start preparing us for sleep.

20:00 Many people eat their main meal of the day around now, though the hormone insulin, which clears digested sugar from the blood, is more effective in the mornings. Some scientists think we should have our main meal at breakfast and only a snack at night.

20:00–22:00 Body temperature and blood pressure fall and we feel more tired. Teens and young adults, however, may continue to feel energetic into the late hours.

02:00 Deepest sleep.

02:00–04:00 Body activity and temperature drop to a low point to conserve energy during sleep. These are the hours in which the very sick or very old are most likely to die.

03:00–05:00 Most births occur around this time. This is true of other primates too. Giving birth in the dead of night may be an evolutionary adaptation that protects the infant, as primates tend to be somewhere safe at night – like up a tree!

FAQ

Can you reset the clock?
The SCN keeps time on its own but is also continually reset by light entering our eyes. The light triggers the release of chemicals onto the clock cells, tweaking it so it matches the 24-hour day. Too little light in the early morning (sunrise) or too much in the late evening (sunset) can upset the clock, putting it out of sync.

Why is it hard getting up?
The cycle of activity controlled by our body clocks changes as we get older. Young children start the day very early in the morning, but between 13 and 21, getting up early and being active in the morning is much harder than at any other time of life. An adult's need for sleep falls with age, making early mornings easier as we get older.

Temperature
One of the main effects of the body clock is to control our temperature, which is 37°C (98.6°F) on average but rises and falls over the course of a day. It peaks between 11 a.m. and 7 p.m., except for a post-lunch dip when we feel sleepy.

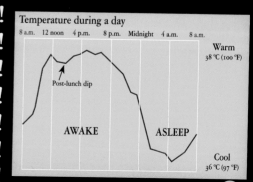

Temperature during a day

8 a.m. 12 noon 4 p.m. 8 p.m. Midnight 4 a.m. 8 a.m.

Warm
38 °C (100 °F)

Post-lunch dip

AWAKE   ASLEEP

Cool
36 °C (97 °F)

day are just BEFORE DAWN

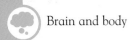

Time *travel*

Why does time fly when you're having fun? An hour spent doing something you love feels like a minute, but a minute spent doing something you hate feels like an hour. The passage of time that we feel – called SUBJECTIVE TIME – is not the same as the time that clocks and watches measure. *It seems to speed up and slow down according to our state of mind.*

WHY DOES LIFE *SPEED UP* AS WE GET OLDER?

One of the reasons that time seems to speed up as we age is that our lives become less varied and active, with fewer new memories to look back on. Another reason is simply that one year of our life becomes a smaller fraction of the total. Using some clever mathematical trickery, a scientist used this declining apparent length of a year to adjust a human life span into subjective years, revealing that by the time we're 10 years old, we're already more than halfway through our subjective life! But don't take it too seriously – the research only made it into the *Journal of Irreproducible Results*, a magazine of scientific jokes.

| 0 | AGE IN ACTUAL YEARS | 1 | 2 | 3 | 4 | 5 | 10 |

| 0 | AGE IN SUBJECTIVE YEARS | 10 | 20 | 30 | 40 | 50 |

SLOWING DOWN TIME

Extreme thrills can slow down subjective time, stretching out each second for longer. This happens because the neurons in the brain's dopamine pathway (see page 68) fire more frequently when we're excited, allowing the brain to process more moments of experience with each second. In car crashes, victims sometimes report that events seemed to happen in slow motion at the moment of crisis. Time also seems to slow down when we're bored or impatient for something to happen – such as the ringing of the school bell at the end a dull lesson.

Time-keeping neurons

Tasks that require an accurate sense of rhythm, such as dancing, depend on special neurons in our brains that keep time. Scientists discovered these in the prefrontal cortex and striatum of monkeys' brains. They fire at specific intervals, such as 10 times a second, and may enable our brains to "time-stamp" memories, allowing us to not only recall events but sense when they originally took place.

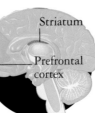

Striatum

Prefrontal cortex

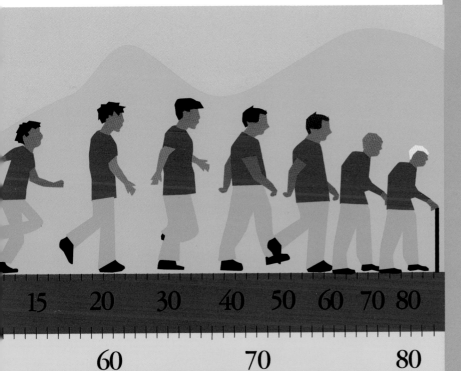

15 20 30 40 50 60 70 80

60 70 80

SPEEDING UP TIME

When your brain is busy focusing on a complicated task, such as playing a tricky level on a computer game, it pays less heed to the passage of time. As a result, time passes without you noticing it and so seems to flow more quickly. Time also seems to move faster if you're rushing to get something finished by a tight deadline.

TIME ILLUSIONS

Now is an illusion

Your brain is very good at making you feel like things are happening *right now*, but that's merely an illusion. It takes about a fifth of a second for an image on your retina to get sent to your brain's visual cortex, recognized, and processed as a conscious experience. As a result, the "now" you experience is always slightly in the past. Fortunately the brain is an expert at predicting what's about to happen from moment to moment, so it always has the right "reaction" up its sleeve and seldom gets caught out by the delay. In fact our brains are so good at predicting that much of what we "experience" is simply what we expect and not what really happens.

Time standing still

We rely on our memory to sense the passage of time through life, but some people suffering from brain damage can lose this ability. One famous patient with this problem, called Korsakoff's syndrome, developed memory loss when he was a young sailor in 1945. For the rest of his life he believed himself to still be a young man and was horrified when he looked in mirrors to see an old man staring back. Fortunately, as soon as he looked away from the mirror he'd forget how old he looked.

SLEEP DISORDERS

Sleepwalking

Do you sleepwalk? It's very common, and may run (or walk!) in the family. Sleepwalking isn't caused by dreaming – it is unconscious movement that happens in the deepest sleep, and you don't remember it in the morning. Some people write, draw, and have even committed crimes in their sleep.

Sleep apnoea

Your body is relaxed when it's asleep, which is the safest state for it – unless you have sleep apnoea, when your throat muscles are so relaxed they collapse and block your airways so you can't breathe. It can be very dangerous, but in most sufferers, their brain wakes them up, usually with a loud snore.

Insomnia

It's normal to wake up a few times during the night, but if you have trouble falling asleep again, it could be insomnia. It's caused by many things, including stress and drinking caffeine. If you find it hard to fall asleep, try to relax before bed (maybe read a book or have a bath), and make sure there's not too much noise or light around you.

Narcolepsy

For some people, it doesn't matter how much they sleep, they want more – sometimes suddenly collapsing into a sleep attack between 30 seconds and 30 minutes long during the day. Narcolepsy can be extremely dangerous: imagine suffering an attack that paralyses you while driving a car.

Sleepy HEAD

We spend one-third of our lives asleep. We know that babies need more sleep than adults, and that teenagers can't get up in the morning, but science doesn't really know what sleep actually does, or even what dreams are for.

TIME FOR BED!

You sleep in a cycle of light and deep sleep that repeats every 90 minutes or so. Brain activity is slowest during deep sleep. During the lightest stage of sleep (REM sleep), your brain creates memorable dreams and is as active as when you're awake. REM stands for "rapid eye movement" – your eyes move around rapidly under their lids in this stage of sleep.

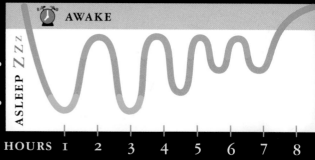

- REM SLEEP
- LIGHTER SLEEP
- DEEPER SLEEP

HOURS 1 2 3 4 5 6 7 8

I don't WANT to go to bed!

EVERYONE NEEDS SLEEP. How much depends on how old you are – the older you are, the less you'll need. While no one knows why we sleep, it's easy to see the effects of too little sleep. If you don't sleep enough, you'll be tired and confused during the day. Continued sleep deprivation will make you feel unwell physically and mentally, causing

WHY SLEEP?

No one's sure what sleep is for, but here are some of the most popular theories.

1 Sleep gives your body downtime – a chance to REST and repair daily wear and tear.

THE STUFF DREAMS ARE MADE OF

Almost everyone dreams. You will have more than 1,800 dreams in an average year, but you won't remember most of them unless you wake up while you're dreaming. Dreams do strange things: they change time – you may feel a dream has lasted hours, but in reality it has taken minutes. Also, dreams feel real – you can't tell that you're in a dream, even if really weird things are happening. Your brain's frontal lobes are mostly shut down when you sleep, so you have no sense of reality.

But WHAT are they *for*?

No one knows why we dream. One theory suggests that it's a way of storing memories; another is that dreams sort experiences from your day. Some dreams are triggered by noises you hear in the night or feelings you have. (Have you ever dreamt of needing the toilet and woken up to realize you actually need to go?) Alternatively, dreams could simply be your own imagination working overtime.

What a *nightmare*

Dreams can feel very scary. This is because the part of your brain that produces emotions is very active when you're asleep. Sometimes it creates a sense of fear, which the rest of your brain weaves into an upsetting dream – a nightmare.

Going without

In 1959, American DJ Peter Tripp broke the then-world record for staying awake. He chatted, played records, and was kept awake by nurses and doctors for 201 hours (8 days). But after just a few days, he began to hallucinate, imagining cobwebs, mice, and kittens, and looking for money that wasn't there. He never fully recovered from the sleep deprivation, and became aggressive and paranoid.

Zzz

vision and speech problems and lowering your immune system. And if you don't sleep at all – not even a nap – for several days, you will die. No one knows how many days of sleep deprivation will kill you because humans haven't been tested. However, rats that were tested died sooner from lack of sleep than lack of food.

2 Sleep allows the chemicals in your brain to **BALANCE OUT** while you're not actively using it.

3 Your brain needs time to build **NEW CONNECTIONS** and process information, storing it in your memory.

4 Being tucked up in bed asleep is a way of avoiding the **DANGERS** of the night.

 I think *therefore* I am

"I think therefore I am", said the philosopher René Descartes about 400 years ago. Descartes had realized that the mere act of thinking was proof of his own existence. Just like Descartes, all of us have a powerful sense of an *inner self* that exists within us and has thoughts, feelings, and sensations. That sense of self is a crucial part of a mysterious human phenomenon we call CONSCIOUSNESS. Our inner self is also utterly unique. Our minds are built and shaped by a set of genes and experiences that are ours alone, giving each of us a *unique personality*.

I think therefore I am

The *curiosity* that is CONSCIOUSNESS

Pay attention!

Can you feel your socks on your feet? The conscious mind is very good at focusing on one thing at a time – a bit like a mental spotlight – and ignoring everything else, such as the sensation of socks on feet. We call this mental spotlight *attention*. You can choose to focus your attention on something, such as this book, but certain things can capture it against your will. If a mouse scurries across the floor in the corner of your eye, or if you hear someone mutter your name, your attention will move in a flash.

The mirror test

Do animals have consciousness? It's impossible to answer this question as we can't get inside animals' minds to look. However, there is a way of testing whether animals might be self-aware. The test simply involves putting a dot of red paint on an animal's face and showing it a mirror. If the animal recognizes itself, it will touch the red dot. Human beings pass this test from the age of 18 months onwards. Only a few animal species pass, including chimps, dolphins, magpies, and (in a variation of the test) pigs – all animals we think of as being intelligent.

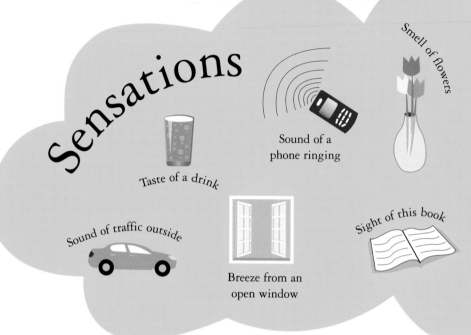

Sensations

Taste of a drink

Sound of a phone ringing

Smell of flowers

Sound of traffic outside

Breeze from an open window

Sight of this book

Consciousness is a

What is consciousness?

When you're in a deep sleep, consciousness VANISHES. When you wake up, it SWITCHES ON like a light, making you aware of the world. Although we all experience consciousness, it's difficult to say what it *actually is*, and even scientists can't agree on a meaning. That's one of the reasons it's such a puzzle.

Think of consciousness as a movie playing in your head. The movie includes not only sound and pictures but smells, tastes, and sensations. There's more still: consciousness includes a secret INNER WORLD of thoughts, feelings, and wishes. Right now, you might even hear the words on this page being spoken by an INNER VOICE. It might sound a bit like a another person, but at the same time, you know it's *you*.

This SENSE OF SELF is an important part of human consciousness. We all feel as though there's a secret inner self living inside our heads, making decisions.

Every moment you are awake, something mysterious is happening in your brain. The information you get from your senses, the thoughts you have, your ideas, feelings, and memories all come together to form *consciousness*. Understanding how it works is one of the big mysteries of science.

Thoughts and feelings

Worrying about exams

Feeling bored

Z Z Z Z

Thinking about clothes you want to buy

sense of *awareness*

Unconscious processes

We like to think we have conscious control of our minds and bodies, but lots of things are beyond our conscious control or even beyond our awareness. You don't have to make a conscious effort to breathe or blink, for instance, though both these processes are controlled by your brain.

Your heart beats nonstop, speeds up, and slows down automatically.

Your lungs pump air nonstop without you having to think about it.

Sensations that don't matter, such as the feel of socks, disappear from consciousness.

Complicated muscle movements become almost unconscious when you've learned a skill such as tying shoelaces.

Where does it happen?

As far as we can tell, there isn't a specific part of the brain that creates the sense of consciousness. Brain-scanning studies reveal that many areas of the brain's cortex are crucial in creating consciousness but none of them can do it on their own. Some people believe that the conscious mind is separate from the physical universe – a kind of spirit or soul. Most scientists, however, think consciousness is simply the result of brain activity.

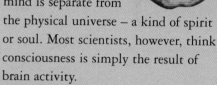

Conscious or not?

Serious head injuries that damage the brain can cause people to stay deeply asleep for days or weeks, a state known as a coma. In some cases, patients wake again but are completely unresponsive, as though they have lost all awareness. Such people are said to be in "persistent vegetative state" (PVS), but are they conscious? Scientists recently scanned the brain of a woman in PVS while asking her to imagine playing tennis. The scan showed the same brain activity as in healthy people thinking of tennis, suggesting that she truly understood and responded to the question.

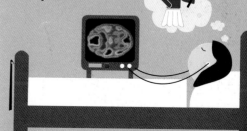

THINKING *without*

SIXTH SENSE

Ever had an odd feeling that something wasn't right *but you couldn't say why?* Perhaps you went to you room and felt something was wrong... A few seconds later, you realize a poster is missing. This is your unconscious mind at work. Without you even noticing, your brain takes in a lot of information and makes a super-fast assessment. If there's a problem, first of all it sends a warning signal to the emotional part of your brain, creating that "something's up" feeling.

Conscious thinking is the tip of an iceberg – just a small fraction of what goes on in our brains. Most mental activity is unconscious, happening behind

First impressions

We rely on unconscious thinking to size other people up. Within a few seconds of meeting someone for the first time, we've jumped to all sorts of conclusions and immediately sensed whether we trust them, though we're often unable to say why. Even the size of a person's pupils can strongly affect our reaction to them: larger pupils make people more attractive.

Unconscious thinking

... or ESP, sixth sense, gut instinct...

If you get bitten by a rat, the you will instinctively avoid it, even

Analysis paralysis?

Is it better to think things through slowly and carefully, or go with your gut instinct and make a snap decision? Imagine you're comparing three new phones, each with loads of different features. Weighing up all the options consciously is extremely difficult, so most people go with their gut. Dutch psychologists have found this often leads to the right answer. They carried out experiments in which people had to use 12 facts to choose the best car from a group, and discovered that people made sounder decisions when they were distracted and unable to focus consciously.

THINKING

the scenes and beyond our awareness. This unconscious processing can be amazingly powerful and fast, but it can also make mistakes.

THE POWER OF INTUITION

We call our ability to think unconsciously "intuition". People with lots of experience develop a strong sense of intuition. In one case, a fire chief in a burning building had a gut feeling something was wrong and ordered his crew out; seconds later the floor collapsed into the basement, where the raging fire had started. The chief put his hunch down to ESP (extrasensory perception), but the truth is that experience had honed his instincts.

The more experience you have, the greater your sense of intuition = intuition...

next time you see one

if you can't remember why

Priming

Intuition isn't always right, and experiments have shown that unconscious thinking can be swayed by trivial or even irrelevant things, an effect known as priming. For instance, people have been found to clean a room more thoroughly just because they could smell disinfectant, or to play games involving money more competitively just because they saw a briefcase in the room. In one recent study, it was found that students rated nonsensical articles about the brain as reliable simply because the articles were accompanied by pictures of a brain scan, while students given the same articles with graphs instead of brain scans found them unconvincing.

Free to CHOOSE?

When we make decisions, we feel as though an inner self is using free will to make a choice. But this may just be an illusion. Ingenious experiments suggest that unconscious parts of our brains make decisions for us up to *10 seconds before* our conscious mind is aware of deciding. In one experiment, a person presses a button whenever they wish while watching letters flash on a screen, noting the letter that's visible when they decide to press the button. Brain scans detected the neural activity that led to the finger movement 10 seconds before the chosen letter appeared. Scientists could even predict the letter the person would choose before they knew themself.

When does he *really* decide to press the button?

Reading MINDS

How do my parents *always*

Be *very careful* if you lie to your parents. They can tell when you're doing it BY PICKING UP ON SUBTLE SIGNALS that you may not realize you're sending out.

1 READING YOUR FACE

Facial expressions give away our inner emotions, even when we're trying to hide or suppress them. You may fake a smile to try to look pleased, but if your eyes remain cold and neutral they will give you away. One of the more honest parts of the face is your forehead – crinkled brows show something is annoying you, even when you're trying not to look bothered.

2 FOLLOWING YOUR EYES

One of the easiest ways to find out what someone is thinking about or what somebody wants is to follow their gaze. People look at things they want, giving away what's on their mind. If you try to hide your thoughts by deliberately looking down or away, that may be obvious too.

FURTHER READING...

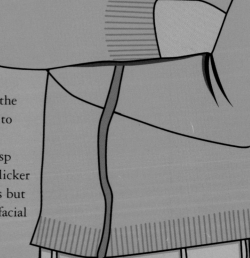

Mirror, mirror

Our ability to read minds may involve special brain cells called mirror neurons. Scientists discovered these by accident in monkeys while studying a part of the monkey brain that activates when a monkey grasps food. The scientists found that the same parts of the brain became active when the monkeys were watching the scientists handle food, as though the monkeys were replaying the sensation in their minds. It's likely mirror neurons exist in the human brain too.

Mirror faces

Mirroring may play a role in the way we use facial expressions to communicate. When we see someone smile with joy or gasp with fear, we not only feel a flicker of the same emotion ourselves but also make the corresponding facial expression to go with it.

According to some scientists, large brains evolved in humans to make us better at UNDERSTANDING EACH OTHER. Success in life requires an ability to figure out what other people think and want – we need to *read their minds*.

know when *I'm* LYING?

③ BODY LANGUAGE

Are your muscles tensed or relaxed? Are your arms folded defensively? We give away a host of clues with our posture and gestures. One subtle form of body language is the way we mirror each other. When we agree with or like someone, we copy their movements; when we disagree or dislike each other, body language falls out of step.

④ INTONATION

The tone of your voice can carry more meaning than the words you actually say. The loudness, pitch, and pattern of breathing all give away your emotional state. Studies have shown that listeners can even figure out how a foreign-language speaker feels without understanding a word they say.

⑤ SELF-AWARENESS

Your parents' main secret weapon is self-awareness. They were once your age and told the same lies to their parents – they know all the tricks. When you try it on, they see their younger selves in you. Their own self-knowledge makes you easy to figure out.

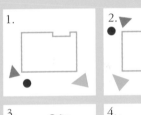
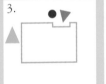

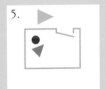

I feel your pain

Watch someone stub their toe and you'll wince in pain too. Watch them make a fool of themselves and you may cringe with embarrassment yourself. We have an amazing ability to step into other people's shoes by experiencing an echo of their own feelings, an ability that helps us read minds. Brain scans even show similar areas of the human brain light up in a person watching someone feel pain as in the person feeling it.

Catching a yawn

Look at the photo and count to ten... Have you started yawning? Yawning is so catching that you can make other people do it without realizing why, simply by standing in front of them and yawning yourself. Why this happens is a bit of a puzzle, but one theory is that yawning is a social signal that tells the rest of the group to get ready for action – by taking a deep breath.

Seeing intentions

Humans beings have a built-in tendency to see intentions in the behaviour of other people or in animals – an ability that helps us predict what other people are going to do. The tendency is so strong that we can even see intention in lifeless objects, such as these coloured shapes. If you read them like a cartoon strip, these images suggest a chase in which the red and purple shapes *run away* from the green shape and *hide* inside the rectangle.

Personality

Are you loud or quiet, tidy or messy? The way you think, act, and interact with others is unique to you and makes up your *personality*. But where does your personality come from – is it set by your genes or moulded by your experience?

What type of person are you?

We all have strong opinions about each other's personality, but our opinions aren't very scientific as they're strongly coloured by who we like or dislike. To assess personality more fairly, psychologists have devised a range of schemes that classify people according to different elements of personality. One of the schemes is shown below. In the middle of each arrow is a question, and at the two ends of the arrows are opposite answers to the questions that different kinds of people tend to prefer. You can use this scheme to take a personality quiz on page 60 and find out a bit more about yourself.

WHAT GIVES YOU THE MOST ENERGY?
Interacting with other people and playing outside.

Having time on your own to concentrate on something.

WHAT DO YOU TEND TO NOTICE?
Important details. Things that are real and actually there.

The bigger picture. Things that you imagine could be there.

HOW DO YOU PREFER TO MAKE DECISIONS?
By thinking things through and weighing up all the important facts.

By thinking about how other people might feel.

HOW DO YOU LIKE TO LIVE YOUR LIFE?
By staying organized and planning what to do next.

By deciding on the spur of the moment and not being too strict.

Find out more about *your own*

NATURE...

Where does your personality come from? Well, you could blame your parents. Scientific studies show that your genes have a big influence on your personality. Identical twins (who share identical genes) who have been adopted into different families grow up with similar personalities despite their different environments. Likewise, biological brothers or sisters are more alike than adopted brothers and sisters.

OR NURTURE?

However, even identical twins don't have identical personalities, so there must be more to personality than genes. Your personality is shaped by your experiences in life (nurture), such as the people you mix with, from members of your family to your friends and teachers. Even what you watch on TV could have an effect on your personality.

The DNA molecule stores genes as a simple code.

Growing up

If you're always in trouble and think your personality is to blame, don't worry. As we grow up, we become much better at understanding our own personalities and those of other people. This knowledge helps us to avoid or to deal with difficult situations such as disagreements. Understanding your own personality can also be a big help in choosing a career that will suit you.

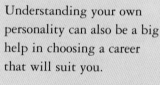

You might be a bit of a wild child, but that won't stop you being a success when you grow up – even if you're still wild underneath!

Multiple personalities

Is it possible to have more than one personality? Some psychiatrists claim to have patients with up to 16 different personalities that take turns to occupy the same body, each with a different name, accent, and no knowledge or memory of what the other personalities get up to. Not all experts are convinced, however. Almost all cases of "multiple personality disorder" have occurred in North America, where films and books featuring the problem have made it famous, perhaps leading psychiatrists to diagnose it too readily or leading patients or criminals to fake the condition.

Testing, testing

The study of personality has involved some very unscientific methods. For centuries, astrologers have used the stars to assess personality, while graphologists study handwriting, but there's no scientific evidence that either technique works. Some psychologists give people ink blots and ask what they can see in them, but many regard this test as unreliable too.

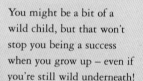

Ink blot

In the novel *Strange Case of Dr Jekyll and Mr Hyde*, Hyde is Jekyll's murderous alter ego (second personality).

I think therefore I am

What are YOU like?

Psychologists use **PERSONALITY** questionnaires to help find out what *kind* of person you are. The questionnaires don't tell you what you **can** or **can't do**, they just reveal how you *prefer to be*. Finding out more about your personality can help you understand **why** and **how** people act *differently* to you.

The questions here can help you identify some of your personality preferences. If you find yourself thinking "I like both the options", try to decide which option seems to describe you best.

? QUESTIONS

1 When you first get in from school what do you prefer to do?
A) Find someone to talk to about your day.
B) Think through your day, maybe in your room while watching TV or listening to music.

2 At school do you prefer to work...
A) In a team?
B) Alone, in private study?

3 When you are given a new board game or computer game would you rather...
A) Read all the rules before you start to play?
B) Start playing and only look at the rules if you need to?

4 Think about a bike. Take a piece of paper and write down what you're thinking. What did you write?
A) A list of facts about the bike, such as its colour, size, what type of bike it is, how many gears it has, if it has lights, and so on.
B) A description that includes where you could go on the bike, how it can get you to places you want to go to, how it is good exercise, and so on.

5 Think about a time that a friend came to you with a problem. Did you...
A) Try to help them by solving their problem?
B) Ask them how they are feeling, say how sorry you felt, put your arm around them, and try to make them feel better?

6 When a friend asks you to read their homework do you...
A) Tell them how they could improve it, so that they will get top marks?
B) Tell them what you like about it and what they did well?

7 Look in your wardrobe. What is it like?
A) Tidy and organized – a place for everything, and everything in its place.
B) A bit of a jumble. You know where everything is but no one else does!

8 When you do your homework, do you prefer...
A) To plan out your work and work until it's finished?
B) To leave it until it really needs to be done, because this is when you do your best work.

IF YOU PICKED As: You may have a preference for *Extraversion* (E). This means you get your energy from being with other people, and may prefer to spend as much time with others as possible.

 IF YOU PICKED Bs: You may have a preference for *Introversion* (I). This means you get your energy from reflecting and thinking through things yourself – so you may enjoy your own company.

Es are sociable and may be frustrated that Is want to spend time alone rather than come out to play. Likewise, Is may be irritated if Es interrupt their thoughts, because Es typically like to talk through their ideas.

 IF YOU PICKED As: You may have a preference for *Sensing* (S). You may prefer your homework to have clear specific instructions. You may enjoy remembering details and facts.

IF YOU PICKED Bs: You may have a preference for *Intuition* (N). You may prefer to see an example of what the homework should look like. You may enjoy daydreaming and using your imagination.

Ss can generally remember lots of details, which may surprise Ns. Ns typically reveal some surprising ideas, so that Ss ask, "Where did that thought come from?" It can be good for Ss and Ns to work together, because then they'll notice all the details and use the information imaginatively.

 IF YOU PICKED As: You may have a preference for *Thinking* (T). This means you prefer to make decisions using logic.

 IF YOU PICKED Bs: You may have a preference for *Feeling* (F). This means you make decisions by considering other people's points of view.

Ts may be seen by others as the ones who typically ask good questions. Fs can often be seen as very thoughtful. When you work in a group to solve a problem or make a decision, it's good to have people with both types of preference.

 IF YOU PICKED As: You may have a preference for *Organizing* (Z). You like to have things planned and well ordered.

 IF YOU PICKED Bs: You may have a preference for *Adapting* (A). You are happy to go with the flow and adapt to the situation.

Zs generally prefer to make decisions as soon as possible, plan things in advance, and know all the information they need upfront. As usually like to leave their options open and decide what to do on the day. They are happy to consider new information as they get it.

JOB CHOICES

People with different preferences can be attracted to different careers. This doesn't mean that if you have one set of preferences, you can't work in a different career – all it shows is that people with certain preferences may enjoy particular jobs. The list below shows some of the jobs that may suit certain types, using the letters from the test as a key.

ISTA	Police officer, sports coach
ISFA	Therapist, dance instructor
INFA	Novelist, translator
INTA	University professor, psychologist
ESTA	Police detective, farmer
ESFA	Nurse, firefighter
ENFA	Social worker, writer
ENTA	Editor, vet
ESTZ	Military officer, manager
ESFZ	Dentist, teacher
ENFZ	Counsellor, actor
ENTZ	Manager, consultant
ISTZ	Airline mechanic, financial analyst
ISFZ	Interior designer, speech therapist
INFZ	Museum curator, architect
INTZ	Chemist, college tutor

THE *feeling* MIND

We often think of the brain as an organ made for *clever things* like THINKING, but it's just as important for creating *feelings.* Whether you're feeling glad, sad, or bad, your brain is to blame. Feelings (*emotions*) well up from deep inside your brain all the time, colouring your *every moment*, even in your dreams, and affecting your WHOLE BODY. The most powerful emotions are basic instincts – drives that push us away from danger and towards the things we *want*.

Emotions

Emotions are intense feelings such as anger and joy that we feel welling up from deep inside us. They affect not just our brain but our whole body and how we act. This is because our most basic emotions are related to primitive survival instincts.

Limbic system

Where do our emotions come from?

Emotions are generated in the limbic system, a cluster of structures deep under the cortex. The limbic system works mostly below the level of consciousness, creating "drives" that push us away from danger and towards opportunities. Intense emotions affect the whole nervous system and feed through to other parts of the brain, making us aware of them, though we don't always know their cause. Emotions have a profound effect on our thinking, swaying decisions even when we're trying to be balanced and logical.

There are six main expressions of emotion and they are exactly the same all over the world. This universal language shows that these emotions are hard-wired into our neural circuits and programmed into us by genes. They happen automatically, and although we can't stop them, we can learn to control or even hide them as we grow older.

JOY

You can tell real joy from fake joy by looking for wrinkles by the eyes ("crow's feet"). The smile affects the whole face and makes the cheeks bulge.

SURPRISE

Surprise widens your eyes, raises your eyebrows, and wrinkles your forehead. Your jaw may also drop – hence the phrase "jaw-dropping".

DISGUST

A look of disgust involves a wrinkled nose, clenched nostrils, pulled-back lips, and narrowed eyes. The look can trigger a sense of disgust in others.

Moods

Emotions are usually short-lived and fade as the body and brain return to their normal state. But if an emotion lingers for hours or even days in the background, we call it a mood. Moods are more vague than emotions: you're either in a good or bad mood, never a "surprised mood" or a "disgusted mood". If a bad mood lasts for weeks or months, it can be a sign of a mental illness such as depression.

Complex emotions

Besides the six main emotions shown below, we experience dozens of more complex emotions such as suspicion, embarrassment, disappointment, guilt, pride, envy, and love. Most of these are concerned with the complexities of human society, and many of them help us to figure out instinctively whom we should trust or avoid.

Crying

Crying is a way of showing sadness and asking for help. Psychologists aren't sure why humans evolved the ability to cry, and as far as we know, we're the only species that does so. One possibility is that crying evolved because it's an honest signal – it's very difficult to shed tears without being genuinely upset or convincing yourself that you're upset.

Can you guess the emotions of the people around you right now?

ANGER

If you're faced with someone who has a fixed stare, lowered eyebrows, tightened lips, and a snarl or clenched teeth, you're in trouble.

FEAR

An open mouth and raised eyebrows can mean surprise, but when you add enlarged pupils, a furrowed brow, and thin lips with a raised upper lip – you're scared!

SADNESS

The sadder a person gets, the smaller their pupils become. When you look at a sad person, your pupils shrink too.

Inside teenage

The **teenage years** can be a *turbulent* time for the brain, as it slowly changes, bit-by-bit, from a TANGLED MESH of connections into an *efficient* network of information superhighways.

PRUNING THE TANGLED BRAIN

In early childhood, millions of new circuits form in your brain's grey matter as neurons connect together in a tangled web of connections. During later childhood and the teenage years, the grey matter thins as the neuronal pathways that aren't used and are no longer needed are "pruned" away.

Stage 1: Synaptic growth

Stage 2: Pruning

Use it or lose it

During what scientists see as a key "use it or lose it" stage, the activities learnt as a teenager – be it playing sports or watching TV – reinforce specific neuronal pathways, while unused pathways are removed. You are left with an efficient brain with less grey matter and more white matter, full of fast neuron highways honed to the well-practised tasks.

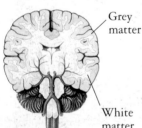
Grey matter

White matter

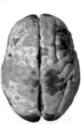
13 years old

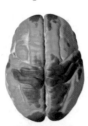
15 years old

18 years old

The red areas show high grey matter volume, with blue and purple showing low grey matter volume.

Moody brain

Teenagers can suffer extreme mood swings and are prone to moments of rash or aggressive behaviour. People often blame these on surging hormone levels, but brain development could be the main culprit. The parts of the brain develop at different speeds. The bits in charge of emotion, rather than thinking, mature first, and these are sometimes in control.

the BRAIN

SLOW RISER

Teenagers find it very hard to get up in the mornings. The teenage brain not only needs about two hours more sleep than the adult brain but also has a very different cycle of daily activity, being most active late in the day and sluggish in the mornings.

PREFRONTAL CORTEX
This area of the brain is in charge of planning, decision-making, and calming behaviour. It is the last part of the brain to mature, and during the teenage years it is remodelled as neuron pathways are pruned.

CORPUS CALLOSUM
This bundle of nerves joins the left side to the right side of the brain. It thickens during your teens and is thought to be involved with creative thinking.

AMYGDALA
This is the emotional hub of the brain and is linked with primal feelings, such as fear and anger. It is one of the areas of the brain that makes teens impulsive.

BASAL GANGLIA
This region includes the brain's reward pathway (see page 68). It generates the "buzz" we experience during pleasure and excitement.

CEREBELLUM
In charge of body coordination, the cerebellum is also thought to play a role in regulating thoughts and learning.

Reckless youth

The age at which you take the most risks is 14. That could be because the 14-year-old basal ganglia are in full working order, giving you the thrill of excitement during risky behaviour, but the prefrontal cortex (the part of the brain controlling decisions) is still maturing, so the brakes are missing. Lacking sound judgement, some teens take crazy risks.

Clumsy brain

The teenage body can seem hard to control at times, with legs and arms growing so fast that the cerebellum has to re-learn how to coordinate them, making the body clumsy. Scientists also think the underdeveloped cerebellum can also make teenagers *mentally* clumsy, making them trip over words and causing moments of forgetfulness.

THE *rewarding* BRAIN

DEEP INSIDE the brain is a special network of neurons dedicated to creating the sensation of **PLEASURE**. These neurons form the brain's **reward system**, repaying behaviour that promotes our survival with a *natural high*.

HOW WE GET A BUZZ

The reward system has certain aims, the most important being to help us survive and reproduce. When we satisfy the urge to eat, drink, or reproduce, we're rewarded with a buzz of pleasure. This encourages us to do the same thing again, reinforcing the behaviour. The pleasure is triggered mainly by the chemical dopamine. Dopamine is a neurotransmitter – a chemical that jumps across the tiny gaps (synapses) between neurons to pass a signal on.

Dopamine is released by a neuron into a synapse and stimulates the next neuron, triggering an electrical signal.

DOPAMINE ACTION

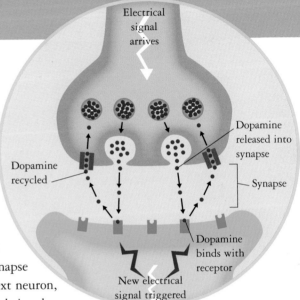

Electrical signal arrives

Dopamine released into synapse

Synapse

Dopamine recycled

Dopamine binds with receptor

New electrical signal triggered

Frontal cortex

Nucleus accumbens

Dopamine-releasing neurons

Ventral tegmental region

THE PATH TO PLEASURE

Dopamine-secreting neurons are arranged in several major pathways inside the brain, one of which is shown here. The pathways start deep inside the brain, where the cell bodies of these neurons are clustered together in areas such as the ventral tegmental region. The neurons' axons (fibres) reach right across the brain, spreading out into the frontal cortex like a fountain to flood the higher brain with dopamine and create the wave of pleasure that we experience consciously.

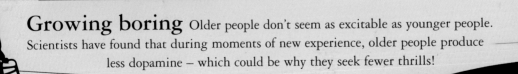

Growing boring Older people don't seem as excitable as younger people. Scientists have found that during moments of new experience, older people produce less dopamine – which could be why they seek fewer thrills!

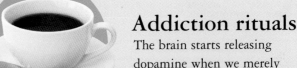

> If I can just press this button again
> I'll forget all my ratty woes...

Dopamine addict

In the 1950s, scientists studying the brain's reward system implanted electrodes into the brains of live rats, allowing the rats to trigger their dopamine pathways using a lever. The rats became so addicted to pressing the lever that they ignored food and carried on pressing until they died of starvation. The research showed that the reward system is so good at reinforcing behaviour that it can cause ADDICTION.

Addiction rituals

The brain starts releasing dopamine when we merely *anticipate* the experience of pleasure, and this anticipation can itself be addictive. Caffeine addicts can develop a fussy ritual over making coffee, from grinding special beans to brewing in a fancy machine. This ritual behaviour triggers a dopamine hit even before the drinker has taken a sip.

Reward chemicals

Dopamine is not the only neurotransmitter that makes us feel good. Lots of other neurotransmitters play a role in how happy or excited we feel, among other functions.

Dopamine
- Pleasure
- Excitement
- Pain
- Nausea

Serotonin
- Happiness
- Sleepiness
- Fullness

Endorphin
- Reduced pain
- Relaxation

Noradrenaline
- Alertness
- Excitement
- Anxiety

Oxytocin
- Love

TOO MUCH OF A GOOD THING

One of the reasons illegal drugs are addictive is that they hack into the dopamine circuit in a similar way to an electrode implanted in a rat's brain (above). Moreover, repeatedly hacking the dopamine pathway causes its effect to fade, driving the addict to take ever-larger doses. A similar thing may happen with junk food. Scientists have found that rats given unlimited high-fat food become addicted to it and get increasingly greedy as the dopamine response in their brains fades. Obesity in humans could be caused by the same mechanism.

> Who you callin' a fatty ratty?

No brakes!

Thrill-seekers love spending their free time doing dangerous things, like leaping off cliffs with parachutes. According to one theory, such people crave thrilling experiences partly because their dopamine neurons work in an unusual way. In most people, the amount of dopamine in synapses is kept in check by special proteins on the surface of dopamine neurons. These proteins, called autoreceptors, act as brakes on the reward system, reducing dopamine release. In some thrill-seekers, however, there are fewer autoreceptors, resulting in a bigger – and more addictive – dopamine kick.

What ARE you

You KNOW when your friends are *laughing*, but would you **recognize** laughter in a remote tribe on the other side of the WORLD? In fact you *would*. Unlike language, laughter is a form of communication that's UNIVERSAL. It's a **basic instinct** that *all people share.* Laughter also does wonders for your mood, increasing blood flow to the brain and releasing pain-killing ENDORPHINS that make you *feel great*.

The *laughing instinct* is programmed into our brains by our genes, but why did it evolve? One clue comes from the fact that we're 30 times more likely to laugh in social situations than when we're alone. Laughter is a form of communication – a way of sending a powerful positive signal to other people in our social group.

Animal crackers

It isn't only humans that laugh. A few other animals that live in social groups – including chimps, gorillas, and dogs – make panting sounds that are like laughter when play-fighting. Unlike humans, however, animals laugh in step with their breaths, whereas we laugh by chopping an outward breath into segments.

WORLD'S FUNNIEST JOKE

According to British pscychologist Richard Wiseman, who collected more than 40,000 jokes from around the world and surveyed their popularity, this is the world's funniest joke:

WHAT'S SO FUNNY?

We all laugh at a good joke, and sometimes at a bad one too. But what exactly is it that makes something funny? Psychologists have tried to dissect our sense of humour and find the funny bone. Here are their best theories about what gets us laughing...

THEORY 1: INCONGRUITY

I said to the gym instructor, *"Can you teach me to do the splits?"* He said: "How flexible are you?" I said: *"I can't make Tuesdays."*

Most jokes involve something incongruous, which means out-of-place and unexpected. The typical joke sets up a situation that seems normal, but the punchline delivers surprising new information that overturns everything, creating a feeling of surprise that makes you laugh.

LaUgHiNg at?

Laughter and bonding

Laughter is a signal that strengthens social bonds. Most primates bond by grooming each other's fur, but humans are different – we use conversation and laughter. Studies have found that the most powerful person in a group often uses humour most, perhaps as a way of commanding loyalty. In tricky social situations, laughter may serve to ease tension, deflect anger, of just fill an awkward silence.

The dark side

Laughter is not without its dark sides. Although it's usually an expression of pleasure, laughter is often used to express aggression. Sharing a private joke about someone can be a way of plotting behind their back, and making a joke about someone in public is a way of ridiculing them and undermining their status.

Even darker – but thankfully very rare – is the potentially deadly effect of uncontrollable laughter, which has been known to trigger a fatal heart attack.

HE HAD THE LAST LAUGH!

Are you ticklish?

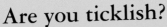

Try tickling yourself – it won't work. Tickling only makes you laugh if someone else is doing it. This is because tickling, like joking, is a form of social communication. Some scientists think tickling evolved from play-fighting, an activity that many mammal species engage in.

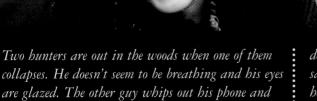

Two hunters are out in the woods when one of them collapses. He doesn't seem to be breathing and his eyes are glazed. The other guy whips out his phone and calls the emergency services. "I think my friend is dead!" he gasps. "What can I do?" The operator says, "Calm down – I can help. First, let's make sure he's dead." There's a silence, then a shot is heard. Back on the phone, the guy says, "OK, now what?"

THEORY 2: **SUPERIORITY**

A woman goes into a cafe with a duck. She puts the duck on a stool and sits next to it. The waiter comes over and says: *"Hey! That's the ugliest pig that I have ever seen."* The woman says, "It's a duck, not a pig." And the waiter says, *"I was talking to the duck."*

Many jokes work by making someone appear silly. Psychologists think we enjoy such jokes because we feel momentarily superior, and that feeling of superiority is so good it makes us laugh.

THEORY 3: **RELIEF**

You're watching a scary movie: a girl is alone in her room at night, slowly brushing her hair. It's so quiet you can hear everything – including the faint footsteps behind her. A hand reaches out, clasps her shoulder, and she shrieks – but it's her mum! According to the relief theory, we laugh after a dangerous moment has passed as a way of reassuring each other that there's nothing to be scared of.

BOO!

FAQ

Can money buy happiness?

The answer depends on whose research you believe. Economists reckon that if everyone's income rises, so does their standard of living and so does happiness. But some research shows that rising wealth in the USA has given no long-term boost to happiness. Some psychologists think that having more money than the people around you or more than you had previously can make you happier, if only for a brief while.

Where's the happiest country?

One psychologist carried out a survey involving thousands of people all over the world and used it to make a "world map of happiness". His research showed that wealthy countries tend to be happier, but happiness is more closely related to health than money, and good education is about as important as wealth. Some poor countries scored highly, such as Bhutan (8th happiest country) – perhaps its strong sense of community and national identity helped. According to the survey, the world's happiest country is Denmark.

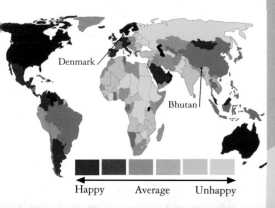

Denmark

Bhutan

Happy   Average   Unhappy

What MAKES

HAPPINESS is like a *sunrise* inside the brain, but how it happens still lies shrouded in a fog of mystery. Are we *born* happy because of our GENES? Does **HAPPINESS** depend on random circumstances? Or can we *choose* to make ourselves happy?

THE SCIENCE OF HAPPINESS

According to one study by psychologists, 50% of the variation in people's happiness can be explained by genes. This suggests that people can indeed be born happy – lucky for some! About 10% of the variation in happiness is due to life circumstances we have little control over, such as our age, where we live, who we share our home with, and the weather. The last 40% is the bit we can control by making day-to-day decisions, such as how to spend our free time and how to treat other people.

How do we know happiness is largely genetic? Studies of identical twins adopted at birth and brought up apart reveal they have a similar level of happiness despite their different circumstances.

50% IS INFLUENCED *by our genes*

us happy? :-)

BORN MISERABLE?

If some people are born happy or born miserable because of their genes, does that mean they're always going to be that way? Not at all. Genes don't *determine* our outlook on life, they simply *influence* it (though possibly rather a lot). To put it another way, if you're born a grouch, you're not *certain* to stay a grouch, you're just *likely* to stay a grouch. And that's good news, so cheer up!

10% due to random CIRCUMSTANCE

40% IS OURS TO control

THINK A LITTLE

UK psychologist Richard Wiseman carried out a survey to see if simple strategies can boost our happiness. He randomly assigned 26,000 people to five groups and asked members of each group to carry out a particular task each day. These were: smile; express gratitude for something good in life; carry out an act of kindness; think about a pleasant event from the day before; or just think generally about the day before (the "control" group). The biggest rise in happiness was among people who thought about a pleasant event the day before. Performing an act of kindness actually made people less happy than the control group.

FAQ

Go with the flow

When we're totally absorbed in an activity we enjoy, whether it's playing a guitar, surfing a wave, or solving a maths problem, we find ourselves blissfully unaware of anything else. That's the theory of Hungarian psychologist Mihaly Csíkszentmihályi. The magical state, which he calls "flow", requires just the right combination of skill and difficulty:

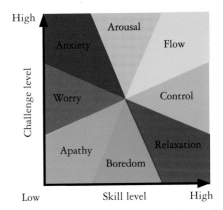

Is the mid-life crisis real?

Research suggests that we're happiest when we're young or old but least happy in middle age. This might be because people have to juggle the demands of stressful jobs and families during middle age. Or it might be that our careers become repetitive and less challenging after a number of years. At least there's a happy ending!

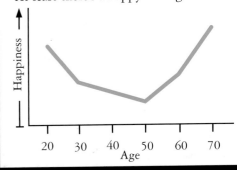

 5 Be physically active. Exercise causes the brain to release chemicals that make you feel good.

 6 Get enough sleep. Too little will make you gloomy and irritable.

 7 Nurture relationships with people that care about you.

8 Focus on helping others, not just yourself.

9 Keep a diary of good things that happen to you.

10 Follow a religion. Religious people are reported to be happier.

 BRAIN *power*

The human brain is a true *miracle*. More powerful than any computer (well... for the time being), it's capable of impressive feats that no animal brain can pull off, from transmitting thoughts by converting them into the coded sounds we call LANGUAGE to *inventing* spaceships, writing heartbreaking music, or figuring out how it came to exist. Your brain has ASTONISHING POWERS whether you know it or not. You just have to learn to *harness* them.

Mind *your* LANGUAGE

The *human brain* is UNIQUE: its left hemisphere specializes in dealing with *language* – something only humans have.

Goo goo, babble babble, mmbarr?

You don't understand!

Language requires several parts of the brain. Wernicke's area deals with meaning. It allows you to understand speech and it gives meaning to your words. To speak, you also need Broca's area, which generates the sequences of instructions to make speech sounds. Babies learn to understand speech before they can produce it, which can make them very frustrated when they can't express what they want to say.

Broca's area

Wernicke's area

BABY TALK

Babies begin to respond to speech before they're born, and as soon as a baby is born it can distinguish its mother's voice from all other sounds. Babies start to babble from around 5 months old, using phonemes (the sounds that make up language). At this age, babies all over the world sound alike. This changes by 1 year old, when the baby's range of sounds has narrowed to only those used in its native language.

PASSING ON THE MESSAGE

Speech is the most common form of communication, but there is a surprising variety of other ways of getting your point across.

Reading words on a page or computer screen that someone has *written* is a common way of learning.

Facial expressions and body language can reveal what a person really thinks.

Universal grammar

The American linguist Noam Chomsky developed the theory of "universal grammar". He noted that children everywhere pick up the complicated rules of language (grammar) once they are exposed to speech. Therefore, he claimed, we must be born with the patterns of language encoded in our genes.

It's easier to learn a second language as a child than as an adult. The "critical period" for learning language ends around 13–20 years old. Late learners may become fluent but probably won't ever master the accent.

Children who grow up hearing more than one language at home can become bilingual (use two languages) with little effort. They will also find it easier to learn additional languages in the future.

What on Earth is she saying?

How many languages can you speak?

Brain-imaging shows that people who learn two languages at once use the same part of the brain to understand and speak those languages. People learning a second language later in life often learn it in a different way using different brain areas.

I CAN'T UNDERSTAND EITHER OF YOU. I'M GOING TO SLEEP.

Use it or lose it

If parts of your brain are not used, their function may be lost forever. In the 1960s an American girl called Genie grew up locked in a room by cruel parents, unable to speak to anyone. Genie was rescued when she was 13 but failed to learn to speak. She could hear and learn single words but couldn't speak in sentences. Although Genie may have had learning difficulties from the start, some scientists think she failed to learn language because it was too late for the unused parts of her brain to develop.

Braille is a system of raised dots that represent letters, which blind people read with their fingers.

Sign language is used in conversation with deaf people, who might also **lip-read**.

How does your *memory* work?

Memory holds everything we know and all we've ever done, whether we can recall it or not. It is highly *organized*: short-term memory briefly stores things we see, hear, or think about; and long-term memory stores the things that we never forget.

SHORT-TERM MEMORY

Short-term memories are made to be forgotten quickly, so they don't clutter our brains. One type of short-term memory, called "working memory", works like a notepad on which the brain stores information from the senses for only as long as we need it. A phone number, for instance, is held in working memory as an imagined sound. To keep it on the notepad, we repeat the sound of the numbers in our heads in sing-song fashion. As soon as we've dialled the number, the memory fades.

Very few people can remember

The magical number

Your long-term memory may be **vast**, but your short-term memory is tiny. Most people can briefly remember only **seven** "chunks" of information, making phone numbers longer than seven digits hard to recall. One way to boost short-term memory is to "chunk" information more efficiently. It's easier to remember "eighteen twelve eleven" (three chunks) than "181211" (six chunks).

Tip of your tongue

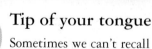

Sometimes we can't recall a word but feel as though we're just about to remember it, saying it's "on the tip of my tongue". One theory for why this happens is that links between the memory of the word and connected memories that help us recall it become damaged or blocked, like a road block in a city. With a bit of effort, we can usually "find a way round" and recall the word.

Smelly old memories

Have you ever sniffed something and suddenly recalled a place you'd forgotten? Smells can excite very powerful memories. The reason is that the parts of the brain that process **smells** are near the hippocampus, which is our memory gateway, and the amygdala, which handles emotions, so a smell can bring back memories and **emotions** at the same time.

LONG-TERM MEMORY

Remembering facts, people, and past events involves our long-term memory, which can last for life. We know this is separate from short-term memory thanks to studies of people with different kinds of *amnesia* (memory loss). Some people with amnesia can remember the distant past but have trouble recalling new things. Others have perfect short-term memory but struggle to recall the past.

What are memories made of?

Memory is a spider's web of connections between brain cells right across the brain. When you experience something, certain brain cells *fire* at the same time so that they learn to fire together and become LINKED. When you recall the experience, these same cells fire again, giving you back the sensation from when you first stored the memory.

The memory gate

Things you see, hear, or learn start off in your short-term memory and trickle into your long-term memory through a kind of gateway, called the **hippocampus**. We know this because of a famous medical patient called Henry Molaison (known as "H.M."). Molaison suffered severe epilepsy, so he had brain surgery and his hippocampus was largely removed. His short-term memory was fine (he could still do crosswords), as was his long-term memory (he could remember his childhood), but information could no longer move from short- to long-term memory and he couldn't remember new things or people, even if he saw them many times a day.

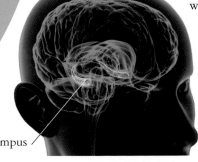

Hippocampus

anything from before the age of three

Déjà vu and jamais vu

Emotions and memories are linked, so when you remember something it feels familiar. If something feels familiar but you don't remember it, that's *déjà vu*. It happens when our brains give us the familiarity alone, without the memory that goes with it. *Jamais vu* is when we remember things that don't feel familiar. If you say a word 30 times quickly, it will become unfamiliar, causing *jamais vu*.

Bad memories

People who go through horrible experiences such as war can get terrible flashbacks for years afterwards. This is called post-traumatic stress disorder (PTSD). The brain protects us by blocking out these really bad memories. But a sudden shock (such as the sound of a car backfiring) will trigger both the memory (gunfire in a war) and the awful emotions that went with it.

Can you change your brain?

Our brains can improve with exercise. Scientists studied the hippocampus of taxi drivers and found that parts of it had grown larger. As well as moving information between short- and long-term memory, the hippocampus helps us work out maps and where things are, which cabbies do all day.

SUPER
memory

People often say their memory is *like a sieve*, but nothing could be further from the truth. If you live to the age of 80, you'll experience over 29,000 *different* days, yet you'll probably be able to REMEMBER many of them quite clearly and vividly. Most of us have super memories — and some people have really astonishing ones.

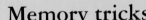

Memory champions

In 2005, Japanese man Akira Haraguchi set a world record by correctly reciting the mathematical number **pi** (an infinite number, beginning with 3.141..., whose digits never repeat) to 83,431 digits. The following year, 11-year-old Indian boy Nischal Narayanam (right) earned a place in the *Guinness Book of Records* by memorizing and recalling 225 random objects in only 12 minutes. Later, he earned himself another record by remembering a 132-digit number in just one minute.

Memory tricks

Memory champions make links between bits of random information so they can recall them later in the right order. "Mnemonics" are rhymes or phrases that link boring facts, such as spellings, into something more memorable. For instance, you can remember how to spell mnemonic with this mnemonic:

*M*onkey *N*ut *E*ating *M*eans
*O*ld *N*utshells *I*n *C*arpet

Another memory trick is to link objects to places. Imagine putting the objects at certain points along a *familiar walk*. Then you can recall them, in order, simply by retracing your steps in your mind.

Stephen Wiltshire

British artist Stephen Wiltshire has been drawing detailed panoramas of cities since he was eight. The amazing thing is that he works entirely from his "photographic memory". He can draw an accurate, 6 m (20 ft) long picture of a city after a single ride in a helicopter. Stephen has autism and did not speak fully until he was nine, but he has an exceptional memory. He became famous at 13 when he appeared on TV, and his paintings now sell for thousands of pounds.

3279502884 19716939...

Give yourself super memory

Ever worried you won't be able to remember everything for your school exams? ***Don't panic.*** There's a brilliant technique that will boost your memory and make your exams a breeze. Research shows that when you learn something new from books or lessons, you'll forget more than half of it within days. But if you spend a few minutes reviewing the information a week or so later, your ability to recall it is vastly improved. If you build weekly reviews into your revision programme when swotting for exams, your brain will commit the facts to long-term memory and you'll remember them for life. The technique works for learning everything from French verbs to the biology of plants.

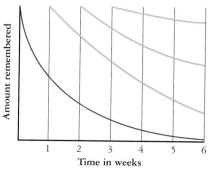

Green lines: amount remembered with weekly reviews.

Red line: amount remembered with no reviews.

TEST your *memory*

Try out these games to test the capacity of your short-term memory for storing **numbers, words,** and **visual** information. What will you remember best?

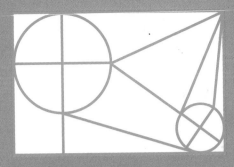

An artistic eye
STEP 1 – To test your memory for visual detail, study the picture above for two minutes, then cover it up and try to draw it from memory. When you finish, give yourself a point for every line you got right.

Visual memory
How good is your memory for images? Study these 12 pictures for 30 seconds, then close the book, wait a minute, and write down as many as you can. How did you do?

You've done well if you remembered more than half of them, and more than 9 is excellent! Now test your memory for words in the game opposite...

We hold **LONG** numbers in our heads by *remembering* their

NUMBER CRUNCHER
Numbers can be harder to remember than words or images. Give yourself 15 seconds to memorize the numbers on the right, then close the book, wait a minute, and see how many you can write down...

201290

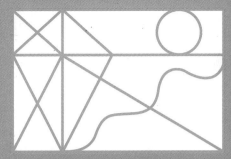

STEP 2 – Now do the same with the picture above, but this time look for familiar shapes in the lines. (Does it look like a picture of a kite with the Sun?) After two minutes cover up the picture and try to draw it from memory. Work out your score again and compare it with your previous one.

You probably did better in the second test than the first because associating the lines with familiar shapes makes them easier to remember.

Did you know you have a photographic memory?

Get a friend to test you with some old photographs (40–50 is a good number). Ask them to keep five of the photos hidden to one side, noting what they are. Look through the main pile of photos quite quickly, spending a few seconds on each one. Ask your friend to shuffle the hidden five photos into the pile, then look through it again. Can you pick out the new photos?

You should be able to pick out the new photos quite easily. You'd struggle to describe what all the images were, but your brain must be storing information about each one of them or you wouldn't be able to tell the old photos from the new.

Carrot   Glass

Armpit   Elephant

Pillow   Trumpet   Flower

Turtle   Nose   Chocolate

Moon   Stone

Word power

Study the 12 words above for 30 seconds. Close the book, wait a minute, and try to write them all down. Then check to see how well you did...

If you scored more than 8, well done! Most people remember words more easily than pictures by using the imagination to create memorable images.

SOUND

Most people can keep only 7 digits at a time in their memory. To help you remember more, try saying the numbers in pairs: 20, 12, 90, 99, 16.

9916

The creative mind

There's more to creativity than painting pictures or playing a musical instrument. The creative mind helps us solve problems and puzzles, and creative thinking has helped scientists to discover new ideas and invent new technologies. Creativity can help you in everyday life too.

During a spot of creative bath-time thinking, Archimedes (257–212 BCE) discovered that you can measure the volume of a gold crown by seeing how much water it displaces.

Eureka moment

Greek scientist Archimedes was in the bath when the solution to a puzzle came to him. He leapt out of the water and ran naked down the street shouting *Eureka*! ("I found it!"). A "eureka moment" – when an idea pops into our head – can happen anywhere: in the bath, in bed, on a bus. Often a change of scenery or a relaxing setting is the trigger, allowing us to see a problem in a new light and hit upon the answer.

How to be creative

The brain works really hard behind the scenes when people are creative. To be inspired and come up with original ideas, the brain has to work through several stages.

WE HAVE A PROBLEM!
The first stage of creative thinking is to realize and understand the problem. In this case, how to cross the river.

BEHIND THE SCENES
You're not aware of the second stage happening. Your brain keeps mulling over the problem, even when you are thinking about other things.

LATERAL THINKING
The key to being creative is not to think *logically* but to think *laterally* – or sideways. Test your creative powers with these lateral-thinking puzzles.

1. It's spring. You see a carrot and two lumps of coal in somebody's garden. How did they get there?

They were part of a snowman, but when spring came the snow melted.

2. A dead man is lying on his back in a field. There are no footprints or tyre tracks, and next to him is a backpack. How did he get there?

The backpack contains his parachute, which failed to open.

3. What's more powerful than God? To give you a clue: the rich need it, the poor have it, and if you eat it you will die.

The answer is the word "nothing".

WAVES OF CREATIVITY

Your brain is buzzing with electrical activity all the time, creating patterns that can be recorded by an EEG (electroencephalography) machine. The wavy lines these machines produce are called brain waves. Creative ideas are most likely to happen not when your brain is hard at work, producing "gamma waves", but when it's relaxed and producing more leisurely "alpha waves". A relaxed state opens up the mind to new possibilities, allowing unexpected thoughts and original ideas to come to the surface.

ALPHA WAVE

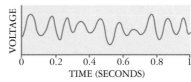

GAMMA WAVE

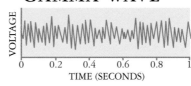

③ EUREKA!

This is the "light-bulb moment" when you hit on a great idea. Often the answer seems to come out of the blue, when you're thinking about something else.

④ MAYBE NOT...

Stage four is when you develop the idea. What at first looks like the best idea in the world may actually be useless. Great ideas are borne out of rejecting the rubbish and improving the good bits.

⑤ PROBLEM SOLVED!

The final stage is testing to see if the idea works. If you've gone through all the right stages, then this is when an idea really comes into its own. (Unless you're a very heavy elephant using a very weak tree...)

MAD GENIUS?

The highly creative mind shares some features with the mind of the mentally ill. A strong imagination, openness to new ideas, and lateral thinking are all helpful in creative thinking, but they are also common symptoms of mental disorders. So what's the difference? A sane person knows that their wild ideas are imaginary, but a person suffering from mental illness may confuse reality and imagination, resulting in delusions. A touch of mental illness can sometimes be a good thing though – some of the greatest thinkers and artists of history have suffered from mental illness.

ISAAC NEWTON

The brilliant scientist Isaac Newton (1642–1727) discovered the law of gravity and the laws of motion, yet he suffered from mental illness throughout his life. It is thought Newton may have had a condition called bipolar disorder, which causes swings of mood from severe depression to high excitement.

Test your *thinking* POWERS

WHAT'S IN A NAME?

Mary's mum has four children.
The first child is called April.
The second is called May.
The third is June.
What's the name of the
fourth child?

DID YOU GET THE ANSWER RIGHT?

Mary. It's a trick question!

HOW LOGICAL ARE YOU?

You're given four cards, each of which
has a number on the front and a
colour on the back. The visible faces
show a 3, 8, red, and green. Suppose
someone tells you that if a card has an
even number on the front, the back is
red. Which cards do you need to turn
over to see if the rule is true?

*The 8 and the green card. Very few people
get this right. Most mistakenly turn over
the red card, but it doesn't matter what's
on the front of it. The rule says that if the
front is an even number, the back is red –
but it wouldn't be against the rule if the
red card had an odd number. Instead of
thinking purely logically (which the
human brain isn't good at) we
instinctively look for evidence to support
the rule and so turn over the red card.
But we should think like a scientist and
try to disprove the rule. If the number on
the front of green is even, the rule must be
untrue. If the back of 8 is not red, the
rule is untrue. The other cards cannot
disprove the rule so don't matter.*

THE GAMBLER'S FALLACY

Pretend you're going to bet £10
on the toss of a coin. First you
watch the coin being tossed five
times – it's heads every time.
Now it's your turn to bet.
Do you choose heads or tails?

*Most people choose tails,
thinking it's unlikely a
coin would land on heads
six times in a row. But
this is a fallacy (error of
logic) because previous
results are irrelevant. The
odds are exactly 50:50 each time, so
heads is just as good a guess. A joke
told among mathematicians explains
the fallacy. When flying a plane, a
pilot always carries a bomb with him.
"The chance of an aircraft having a
bomb on board is very small," he
reasons, "so the chance of there being
two bombs is minuscule!" (Don't try
this at home – it's just a joke!)*

that our brains jump to conclusions. Even when we're *trying* to be logical, our subconscious mind and our *EMOTIONS* interfere with our thinking and trip us up. See if your thinking powers are good enough to solve these puzzles, but be warned: *they're tricky*!

THE SUNK COST FALLACY

You buy a cinema ticket for £10 a day before going to see the film. When you arrive, you realize you've lost the ticket and the assistant won't let you in. She offers to sell you another ticket for £10, but that will mean you've spent £20 on the film. What do you decide to do: buy another ticket or walk away?

The rational answer is to buy a new ticket. The lost ticket should make no difference to your decision. Just as losing a £10 note the previous day should make no difference. If the film was worth paying £10 to see yesterday, it is still today. This is an example of what economists call the "sunk costs fallacy". (A sunk cost is money that's already been spent.) Another example is watching a terrible film all the way through "to get your money's worth" rather than walking out. Walking out is the rational decision: the money has already been lost — don't waste time on top of it.

FALSE POSITIVES

TRUST ME, I'M A DOCTOR!

Imagine you go to the doctor and take a test for a rare illness that affects only 1 in 200 people. The doctor carries out a blood test that works 98% of the time and tells you the result is positive, indicating you have the illness. What's the chance the test is wrong and you are in fact perfectly healthy?

It's 80% likely that the test is wrong. Does this feel unbelievable? The maths proves it's true. Imagine 200 people take the test. Only one person is likely to have the illness, but the test will (on average) make four mistakes, most likely telling four healthy people they are ill. So there will be five positive results, but only one out of those five is a correct result.

THREE DOORS PROBLEM

1ST PRIZE

Imagine you're on a TV quiz show. Hidden behind one of three doors is a sports car; pick the right door and you win it. You pick a door at random. The quiz show host, who knows where the car is, then opens another door and reveals an empty room. He gives you a chance to change your mind. Should you?

Yes. Your chance of winning if you change your mind rises from one-third to two-thirds. This can be hard to believe because it's counter-intuitive (goes against your gut feeling) — it feels like the chance of winning if you switch should be 50:50, because there are two doors and the car could be behind either one. To see why the answer is two-thirds, work out your chance of losing if you always switch. You would only lose if you'd picked the car at first, so you have a one-third chance of losing if you always switch. Therefore, your chance of winning is 1 minus one-third, which is two-thirds.

STRANGE

When *injury* or *disease* strikes the brain, the consequences can be strange. Like a computer program riddled with bugs, a damaged brain suffers from

Lost in music

Clive Wearing was a brilliant musician until a virus attacked his brain and crippled his memory. Now he suffers from one of the worst cases of amnesia ever recorded: he constantly feels like he's woken from a long sleep and remembers nothing for more than 30 seconds. When his wife leaves the room then returns, he hugs her like a long-lost friend he's not seen for decades. When he meets someone, he'll shake their hand and say, "Are you the King?". Because he can't remember them, he assumes they must be important. Despite his amnesia, he still knows how to play the piano and conduct an orchestra.

Two brains

People with severe epilepsy are sometimes treated with brain surgery that involves cutting their corpus callosum (a cable of nerve fibres between the two halves of the brain that helps them work together). After it's cut, people can behave as if they have two brains. They are able to draw different things at the same time with their two hands. Also, their "two brains" may fight for control, causing something called "alien hand" syndrome. One hand starts doing things the person can't control, like removing their clothes, or their left hand might lift a chocolate bar to the person's mouth while their right hand tries to snatch it away.

Taking sides

For people with spatial neglect, right or left suddenly ceases to exist. The right brain hemisphere helps us see things on the left side of space, and vice versa. If the top part of your right hemisphere gets damaged, you stop noticing things on the left even though your eyes still work perfectly. If given food, you'll eat only food on the right side of the plate.

FACE OFF

Prosopagnosia is one of the weirdest disorders that can hit your brain. It means you suddenly stop being able to recognize people's faces, even though you can still see them perfectly well. People suffering from this disorder have to identify friends and family by their voice, smell, body language, or the clothes they wear. Prosopagnosia doesn't only affect human faces. One farmer with the disease could no longer recognize his cows, while another farmer couldn't recognize people's faces but could recognize his cows and dogs.

BRAINS

very specific *glitches*. These neural errors can shine light on what the various parts of the brain are for.

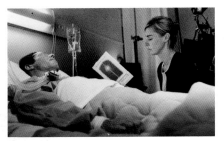
Scene from the film *The Diving Bell and the Butterfly* about Bauby's life.

What can you see?

Nothing, I'm completely blind!

Well have a guess.

Um... then I guess horizontal red stripes??

Locked in

Following a massive stroke in the 1990s, French writer Jean-Dominique Bauby was left suffering from locked-in syndrome: his brain was conscious, but his body was paralyzed. All he could move was his left eyelid. He managed to write a book about his experience by dictating one letter at a time. It took two minutes to dictate each word and Bauby had to blink about 200,000 times to complete the book.

The strange case of the missing brain

About 30 years ago, a very bright maths student in England was referred to a specialist to investigate the cause of a swollen head. The doctor carried out a brain scan and discovered, to his utter amazement, that the boy apparently had no brain. The boy's head was full of water and his cerebral (brain) tissue had been compressed into a thin layer just a millimetre or so thick that lined the inside of his skull. The student was suffering from hydrocephalus ("water on the brain"). Despite his condition, he had an IQ of 126, graduated with a first-class honours degree, and went on to lead a perfectly normal life.

Blindsight

In 1973 an English man underwent surgery to remove a tumour from the visual area in the back of his brain and was blinded as a result. But when doctors assessed his vision, they discovered he could correctly guess what he was looking at despite being unaware of seeing it. The patient was just as astonished as his doctors. It was a fascinating discovery as it suggested that the surgery had destroyed not vision but *consciousness of vision*. Some part of the brain was still processing images from the eyes and seeing.

Body doubles

Two creepy brain disorders are linked to prosopagnosia. People with Capgras Syndrome think their friends or family have been replaced by imposters. Cotard's Syndrome is even more bizarre. Sufferers see a stranger when they look in the mirror and think they don't exist, or they believe they're dead or dying. The two disorders are often caused by brain damage that disconnects the visual parts of the brain from the emotional parts.

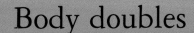

Psychic

HAVE YOU EVER been thinking about an old friend just as they telephoned? Some people claim such experiences are caused by *psychic powers* such as

THE SIXTH SENSE

Psychic abilities are said to happen through a mysterious "sixth sense" that is claimed to give people "extrasensory perception" (ESP).

Telepathy

Telepathy is the ability to read someone's thoughts. One famous example involved psychologist Hans Berger, who nearly died falling off a horse. His sister, far away, sensed he was in danger and sent a telegram. Amazed, Berger decided to study telepathy. His investigations into brain waves (the brain's electrical activity), which he believed carried thoughts into other people's minds, failed to prove telepathy existed but came in useful for all sorts of other brain research.

Clairvoyance

A person who can "see" things in a distant place or in the past or future is said to be clairvoyant. Before the age of satellites, the US and Soviet intelligence agencies both used clairvoyants for spying, but with no success. Up to a third of US police forces have resorted to using clairvoyants to solve crimes, but none say the technique worked.

Telekinesis

Telekinesis means moving objects by the power of thought alone. It's strictly against the laws of physics, but that doesn't stop people having a go. Edouard Buguet (left) faked photographs that showed his supposed ability to levitate objects, but others have claimed to make compass needles move, metal objects stick to their body, or spoons bend and break.

Test your psychic powers

Try this with a friend. You need to:

1. Draw the five shapes (right) on identical pieces of card. These are called Zener cards after Karl Zener, who designed them to carry out scientific experiments on ESP.

2. Shuffle the cards and pick one at random, without showing anyone.

3. Concentrate hard on the pattern and try to beam it telepathically to a friend.

4. Do this 20 times, writing down a numbered list of the cards you've "sent"...

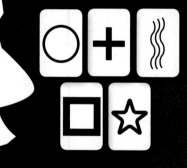

The science of ESP

If psychic phenomena really exist, it should be possible to detect them scientifically. This is what some scientists have tried to do in laboratories set up to investigate "parapsychology". In one typical experiment, scientists ask people to send images of Zener cards (above) telepathically. So far, there's no evidence that the person receiving the thought gets the right answer significantly more often than would happen by chance. One famous sceptic has even offered a prize of $1 million to the first person to show ESP works under scientific conditions.

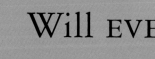

Will EVERYONE who *believes* in

powers

telepathy, but is there any scientific evidence that such things exist? Or are psychic phenomena just a matter of chance, coincidence, and trickery?

Most scientists are sceptical about psychic phenomena. That's because many of them are easily explained.

The power of coincidence

Strange things do happen by chance, but because our brains are programmed to search for explanations and patterns, we have a tendency to overinterpret random events. Imagine a friend rings just as you're thinking about them – you might be so startled that you believe it was telepathy. But how many times did a friend ring when you *weren't* thinking about them? We notice the coincidences and ignore the non-coincidences.

A miracle a month

British mathematician John Littlewood worked out we can expect to witness an average of one miracle a month. Littlewood defined a miracle as a "one in a million" event. Assuming we're alert for 8 hours a day, we experience one million seconds each month, so the average number miraculous seconds each month must be one. Next time you see Jesus on a slice of toast, put it down to the laws of chance.

Confirmation bias

Visit a haunted house and you're *much* more likely to interpret spooky sounds as evidence of ghosts, especially if you already believe in the supernatural. We all have a natural tendency to notice evidence that supports our beliefs. Scientists call this tendency "confirmation bias" and try to avoid it by designing experiments that attempt to *disprove* (rather than prove) their theories.

... Your friend should write down each card too. Tot up the score at the end. By chance alone, your friend is 98% likely to get up to 7 cards right. The chance of guessing more than 10 is less than 1 in 300, and the chance of guessing all 20 is *1 in 100 trillion*. If you do get all 20, congratulations! You're both real psychics!

Tricks of the trade

Psychics use a lot of trickery to read minds and tell fortunes. "Cold reading" involves looking for clues in a person's body language and appearance (a skill we all have). "Barnum statements" are seemingly personal insights that could apply to anyone, such as "I sense you're having problems with a close friend or relative..."

telekinesis please RAISE **MY** *hand*

WILL MACHINES BOOST OUR BRAINS?

Bionic bodies

People are already able to control artificial limbs using the power of thought. Nerves from the limb are connected to motors that make fingers or feet flex. Thinking about an action makes the limb respond.

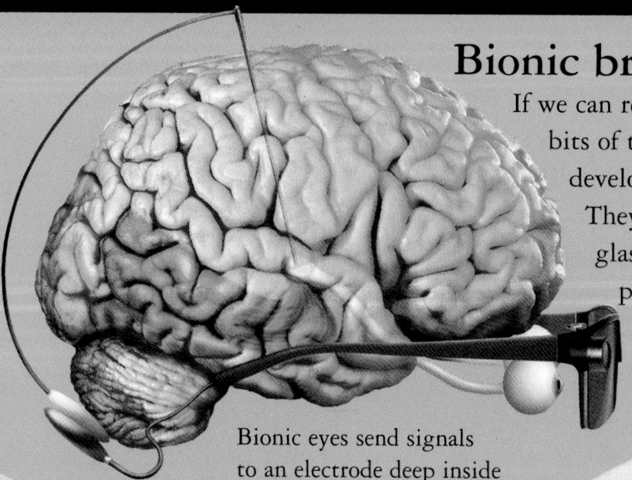

Bionic brains

If we can replace parts of the body, why not bits of the brain too? Scientists have already developed artificial retinas for blind people. They use tiny cameras, mounted on dark glasses, that send signals directly into the person's optic nerve, giving them a crude kind of replacement vision.

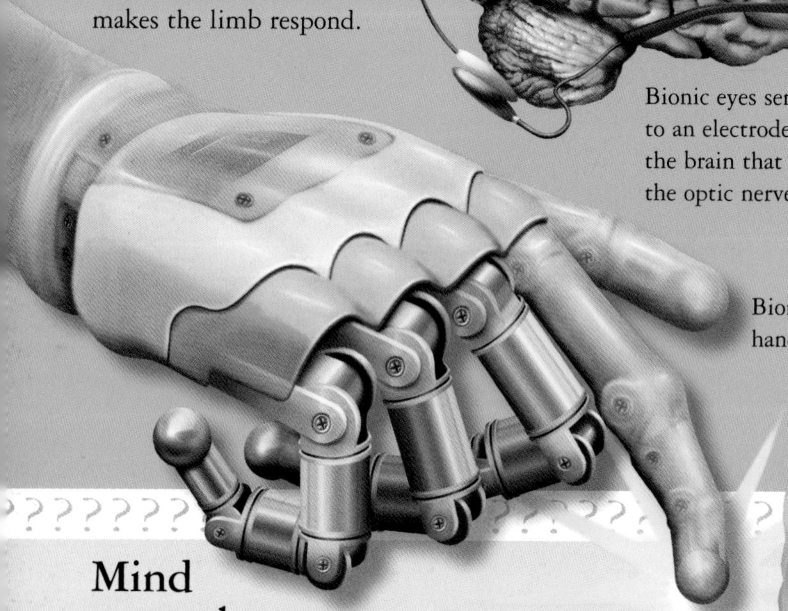

Bionic eyes send signals to an electrode deep inside the brain that stimulates the optic nerve.

Bionic hand

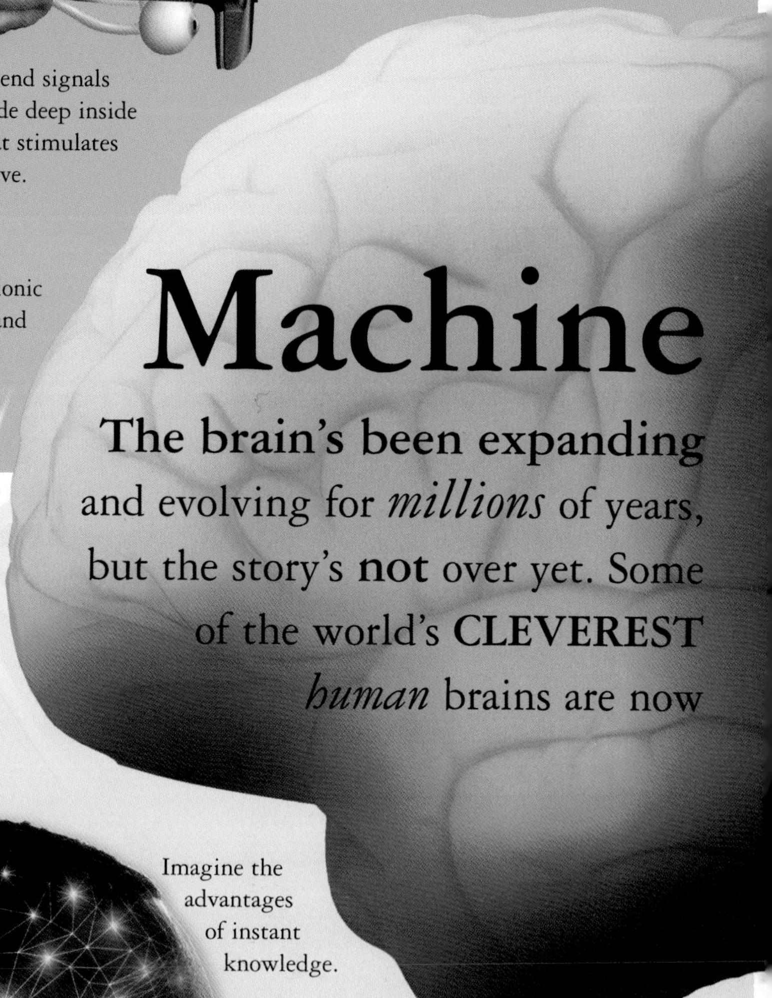

Machine

The brain's been expanding and evolving for *millions* of years, but the story's **not** over yet. Some of the world's **CLEVEREST** *human* brains are now

Mind control

If you hate typing messages into a computer keyboard or mobile phone, you probably can't wait for a gadget that can read your mind. Scientists are testing brain-reading skullcaps and clip-on electrodes that detect brain activity, which may one day allow us to control cars, computers, games, and many other things simply by thinking about it.

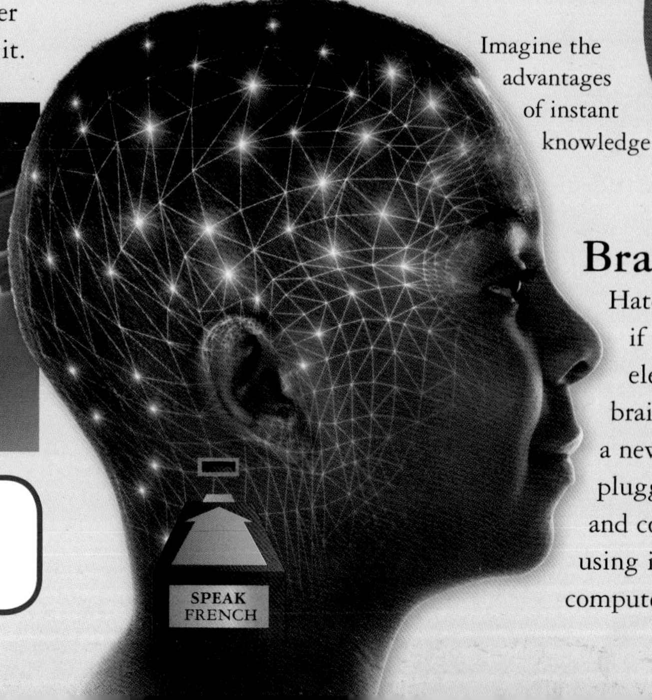

Imagine the advantages of instant knowledge.

I'm playing MINDBALL. If I **concentrate** *really* hard I can make the ball MOVE!

Brainputers

Hate doing homework? What if someone could develop an electronic memory card for the brain that would enable you to learn a new language in seconds simply by plugging it in? In the future, brains and computers could merge together using implants inside your head and computers that work more like brains.

SPEAK FRENCH

WILL MACHINES EVER THINK LIKE US?

Neural networks

One way to make computers more powerful is to build them more like brains. A neural network is a computerized model of a brain made up of artificial brain cells. If information is fed in, it slowly starts to recognize patterns and make connections, just like a human brain. If you show a neural network thousands of pictures of faces of people from France or China, then present it with an unknown face, it should be able to tell you whether it's French or Chinese without being told what to look for. That's very different to an ordinary computer, which has to be told exactly what to do.

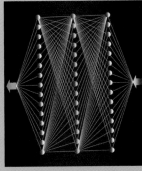

A neural network

A RAT flying a jet? Whatever *next...*

MINDS

developing AMAZING *artificial* ones, opening up astonishing new directions in which *brains* might evolve in the future.

Rat brain flies jet!

It takes a supercomputer the size of a warehouse to make a neural network as powerful as a mouse's brain, but it's much simpler to make an artificial brain from scratch. Scientists have done just that by taking 25,000 rat brain cells and forming them into a tiny neural network. They then wired the rat brain into a microchip and taught it to fly a jet fighter using a flight simulator programme.

The "Interbrain"

Have you noticed how the Internet is turning our planet into a kind of giant brain? It already shows some brainlike behaviour. It can store information and forget (delete) it. The Internet shows anger or excitement when lots of people discuss a hot topic in emails and blogs. It's almost as though the Internet has a mind of its own!

Are we creating a world-wide brain?

Turing test

Computers routinely beat people at chess, but no computer can walk, talk, think, or learn like a human — well, not yet. Scientists have been trying for decades to give computers artificial intelligence (making them think for themselves), but how will we know when they succeed? British mathematician Alan Turing suggested a simple but clever way of checking a computer's intelligence. You sit someone at a screen that's connected either to an "intelligent" computer or another person in a second room. Just by chatting and asking questions, the tester has to discover whether they're talking to a person or a computer. If they can't tell the difference, and it's actually a computer they're talking to, the computer can be regarded as intelligent.

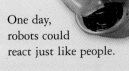

One day, robots could react just like people.

GLOSSARY

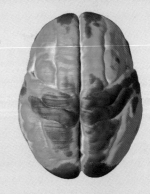

3D Seeing an object in three dimensions means you see its length, width, and height. A cube is 3D, but a square is 2D, because it has only length and width.

amygdala The part of the brain's limbic system that deals with emotions.

axon A long fibre that extends from a nerve cell (neuron). It conducts nerve signals away from the cell.

basal ganglia A region at the base of the front of the brain containing millions of nerves that deals with choosing and controlling movement.

behaviourism A branch of psychology that is devoted to the study of animal and human behaviour but disregards the internal workings of the brain that control behaviour.

bipolar disorder A mental illness in which sufferers experience extreme highs (mania) and lows (depression).

body clock A natural time-keeping mechanism in the body that controls regular cycles such as daily sleeping.

brain stem The part of the base of the brain that connects to the spinal cord.

Broca's area An area in the brain's frontal lobe that deals with speech and producing language.

central nervous system The brain and spinal cord together make up the central nervous system.

cerebellum A part of the brain that helps to coordinate body movements and balance. It is at the base of the back of the brain.

cerebral cortex The folded layer of tissue that forms the outer part of the brain. It's used for thinking, memory, movement, language, attention, and processing information from our senses.

cerebral hemispheres The two halves of the cerebrum: left and right.

cerebrum The main part of the brain not including the brain stem and cerebellum.

consciousness The state of being mentally aware.

critical period A period of life in which the brain has a greater ability to learn new skills. The critical period for learning a second language is in childhood. After this time, it becomes much harder.

dendrite A short fibre that extends from a nerve cell (neuron). It picks up signals from other nerve cells.

emotions Inner feelings that affect both the brain and body, such as joy, fear, disgust, and anger.

endorphin A type of neurotransmitter that blocks pain.

epilepsy A brain disorder that can cause violent physical seizures (fits) resulting from bursts of abnormal electrical activity in brain cells.

ESP (extrasensory perception) Also known as psychic powers or a "sixth sense", a claimed ability to read minds, move objects with the power of thought, or see into the future.

frontal lobe The front part of each cerebral hemisphere. It is involved in higher mental functions, such as making decisions.

grey matter Darker brain tissue that contains nerve cell (neuron) bodies and dendrites.

hippocampus A part of the brain that helps lay down long-term memories.

hormones Messenger chemicals that travel through the body in the blood.

instinct A behaviour that is programmed into an animal from birth and does not need to be learned from scratch.

intuition the use of a hunch or insight to figure something out quickly, without reasoning.

lateral thinking Thinking creatively to solve a problem, using ideas that may not appear logical.

limbic system A group of brain parts that deal with emotions, memory, and the sense of smell. The amygdala and hippocampus are parts of the limbic system.

lobe One of four main divisions of each cerebral hemisphere. Each hemisphere has four lobes: frontal, occipital, parietal, and temporal.

mind The thoughts, feelings, beliefs, ideas, and sense of self that are generated by the brain make up what we call the mind.

mirror neurons Neurons in the brains of monkeys that become active when the monkey watches another monkey or a person doing something. Mirror neurons are also thought to exist in humans and may enable us to feel an echo of other people's sensations.

neuron Another word for a nerve cell. Neurons produce electrical signals when stimulated (made to act by an outside source, such as your senses). They pass the signals to other neurons or to muscles.

nerve cell See neuron.

neurosurgery Medical treatment of the brain involving an operation.

neurotransmitter A chemical created by nerve cells (neurons) that relays nervous signals across synapses from one neuron to another.

occipital lobe The lobe at the back of the cerebral cortex. The occipital lobe processes vision.

parietal lobe A lobe between the top and rear of each cerebral hemisphere. The parietal lobe receives nervous signals from all over the body and helps create the sense of touch.

prefrontal cortex The outer layer of the front of the brain. It deals with conscious thought and planning.

proprioception A sense that keeps us aware of the position and motion of every part of the body.

prosopagnosia A brain disorder that causes people to become unable to recognize faces.

psychology The scientific study of the mind.

REM (rapid eye movement) sleep The lightest form of sleep, during which the eyes move rapidly under their lids. The most memorable dreams take place during REM sleep.

retina A layer of light-sensitive neurons lining the back of each eye. The retina captures images and relays them to the brain as electrical signals.

saccade The movement of the eye as it flicks from place to place.

schizophrenia A mental illness in which hallucinations and delusions give the sufferer a false sense of reality.

senses The five main senses are vision, hearing, smell, touch, and taste. Other senses include pain, proprioception, and sensitivity to heat or cold.

spatial awareness A grasp of shape, distance, and space.

spinal cord A large bundle of nerves down the backbone, connecting the brain to nerve cells throughout the body.

synapse A tiny gap between two nerve cells (neurons).

telepathy The claimed ability to read someone's thoughts through extrasensory perception (ESP).

temporal lobe The side lobe of each cerebral hemisphere. The temporal lobe deals with hearing, language, and memory.

thalamus An area near the base of the brain that assesses incoming information from the eyes and other sense organs.

visual cortex A part of the occipital lobe at the back of the brain that processes vision.

Wernicke's area A part of the temporal lobe that deals with understanding language. In most people it is in the left hemisphere.

white matter Lighter-coloured brain tissue mainly containing axons.

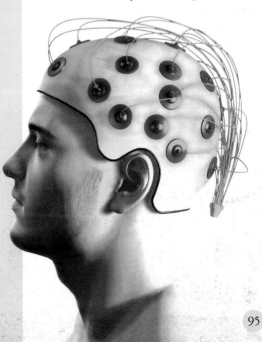

INDEX

Acknowledgements

Dorling Kindersley would like to thank Paul Yarker for helping to devise the personality test and Kathrin Cohen Kadosh for supplying the brain scans on page 23.

The publisher would like to thank the following for their kind permission to reproduce their photographs:
(Key: a-above; b-below/bottom; c-centre; f-far; l-left; r-right; t-top)

Edward H. Adelson: 36c, 36cr; **Alamy Images:** ARCO Images GmbH 71tl; Art Directors and TRIP 71cl, 71cr; Richard Green / Commercial 7cl, 52cl; Interfoto 11c; Andrea Matone 34cr; Patti McConville 90cl; Medicalpicture 92cl, 92tr; David Price 66bl; StudioSource 41bl; Richard Wareham Fotografie 41cr; **The Bridgeman Art Library:** Tretyakov Gallery, Moscow, Russia 30b, 31b; (c) David Macdonald (www.cambiguites.com): 37bl; **Corbis:** Lucas Allen 19 (Book); Bettmann 11br, 11cl, 11tc, 22bl, 22cl, 33tl, 39tl; Bloomimage 52-53bc; Coleen Cahill / Design Pics 42c; Alan Copson 48-49tc; Leonard de Selva 11bl; DLILLC 70cl; Robert Dowling 71bl; EPA/ Toni Garriga 50c; Francis G. Mayer 33c; Frank Lukasseck 19cr; Frare / Davis Photography / Brand X 15bc; The Gallery Collection 10-11b, 33tr, 35tc; Etienne George 89cl; Michael Gore/FLPA 44bc; Sven Hagolani 29tr (TV), 39tr, 78cb; Rune Hellestad 52bl; Ikon Images 79cra; Images.com 48tl; Imagezoo / Images.com 86cr; JGI / Blend Images 27bl; JLP/ Jose L. Pelaez 48bl; Mike Kemp / Rubberball 19 (Rat); Matthias Kulka 18r; Mehau Kulyk / Science Photo Library 54-55cb; Martin Harvey 30tl; Rob Matheson 48-49t; Dan McCoy - Rainbow/ Science Faction 53cr; MedicalRF.com 13bl; moodboard 41t; Louis Moses 49bc; Nice One Productions 79cra; Sanford / Agliolo 49br; Roberta Olenick / All Canada Pictures 69cr; ANDREW PARKINSON 29tr; Herbert Pfarrhofer 12ca; PoodlesRock 4bl; Radius Images 67br; Lew Robertson 69crb; Thomas Rodriguez 79cr; Andersen Ross/Blend Images 79cra; Sanford / Agliolo 49br; David Selman 70bl; Athina Strataki / Etsa 71c; Scott Stulberg 70-71c; Sunset Boulavard 59br; Yuji Tanigami / amanaimages 44bl; William Whitehurst 93bl; Harry Williams 76-77c; **Crytek GmbH:** © 2010. All rights reserved. This picture has been created by Sascha Gundlach using CryEngine®3. 35clb; **Dorling Kindersley: Rachael Grady:** 4bc, 83tr; Tim Ridley / Ted Taylor modelmaker 93cra; **Eyevine Ltd:** 14bl; **Getty Images:** 3D4 Medical.com 13tc; 35br, 77tl; Altrendo 91br; Colin Anderson 4-5b; Chad Baker / Thomas Northcut 92bc; Barcroft Media 80-81tc; Bettmann 15c; Burazin 88cr; Creative Crop 70tl, 71ftr; Peter Dazeley 34tl; De Agostini 7t, 10tc; Digital Vision 47bc; Edvanderhoek 18tl; Shaun Egan 37cl, 37cr; David Elliott 41cla; Daisy Gilardini 46tr; Hulton 12cl, 13c; Hulton Archive 12c; Imagezoo 71tr; David Job 55c; Mike Kemp 8-9, 10ca, 10-11t; Peter / Stef Lamberti 16c; Catherine Ledner 17cl; Lester Lefkowitz 15tr; Loungepark 70cb; Steve McAlister 40t; Ryan McVay 15br, 66-67; Brian Mullennix 88cl; Gary John Norman 17bl; Carl Pendle 60cl; PM Images 41bc; Reza 67tr; Achim Sass 40br; Venki Talath 54bc, 54cb, 54crb; Alan Thornton 69c; Time & Life Pictures 85br; Eric Van Den Brulle 55tr; **Harlow, John M.:** Recovery from the passage of an iron bar through the head. By John M. Harlow, M.D. Read before the Massachusetts Medical Society, June 3, 1868; Boston, David Clapp & Son, 1869 11cra; **iStockphoto.com:** 4x6 68bl; 16tr; Alexsl 62; Andresr 40cr; Andyd 69cr; Cimmerian 81br; Dreamstime 59bc, 59tl; Dreamstime

/ Kts 23tl; EcoPic 56cl; Rebecca Ellis 76cl; Julie Felton 76bl, 89r; Jcdesign 24tc; Sebastian Kaulitzki 2-3, 3c, 88-89t; Jan-Willem Kunnen 91tr; Markus Leiminger 68br; Nancy Louie 7bl, 77cr; Miodrag Nikolic 77b; penfold 10-11ca; TommL 76br; Viorika Prikhodko Photography 16cb; Tomasz Zachariasz 16bl; **David James Killock,** (killock@msn.com) http://www. wix.com/dkillock/dkphotography: 39b; **The Kobal Collection:** 46b; **Nischal Narayanam:** 80b; **NASA:** 34clb; JPL/ Malin Space Science Systems 33tc (Real); The Natural History Museum, London: 14tl, 23br; naturepl. com: Anup Shah 17cr; **Dan Paluska:** 91c; **PNAS:** 101(21):8174-8179, May 25 2004, Nitin Gogtay et al, Dynamic mapping of human cortical development during childhood through early adulthood © 2004 National Academy of Sciences, USA / image courtesy Paul Thompson, UCLA School of Medicine 66c; **Richard Russell, Assistant Professor of Psychology, Gettysburg College, USA:** Russell, R. (2009) A sex difference in facial pigmentation and its exaggeration by cosmetics. Perception, (38)1211-1219. 38tr; **Aaron Schurger:** 32b; **Professor Philippe Schyns:** Schyns, P. G. & Oliva, A. (1999). Dr. Angry and Mr. Smile: When categorization flexibly modifies the perception of faces in rapid visual presentations. Cognition, 69, 243-265, with permission from Elsevier. 38tl; **Science Museum / Science & Society Picture Library:** Science Museum 92bl; **Science Photo Library:** 15cl; AJ Photo / Hop Americain 85t; John Bavosi 44cl; Dr Klaus Boller 5bl; Gary Carlson 21bl; CNRI 42ca; Equinox Graphics 21cr; Gusto Images 54-55ca; Victor Habbick 93crb; Roger Harris 19br, 64c, 79c; Helene Fournie, ISM 28tl; Laguna Design 21tc, 78-79tc; Lawrence Berkeley National Laboratory 20cr; David Mack 31tl; National Library of Medicine 14cl; National Museum, Denmark 10bl; Omikron 28br; Pasieka 4tl, 20cl, 93tc; Sovereign, ISM 23bl, 23c, 23ca; Volker Springel / Max Planck Institute For Astrophysics 5br; Sheila Terry 22c; Geoff Tompkinson 18cl; Jeremy Walker 90tl; Paul Thompson, **UCLA School of Medicine:** 66cr; **University of Leicester:** Adrian White, Analytic Social Psychologist 72bl; **Wellcome Images:** 13cr; **Wikipedia, The Free Encyclopedia:** Bibliothèque nationale de France, département des Estampes et de la Photographie, Paris 90bl; Fibonacci / Permission is granted to copy, distribute and/or modify this document under the terms of the GNU Free Documentation License, Version 1.2 or any later version published by the Free Software Foundation; with no Invariant Sections, no Front-Cover Texts, and no Back-Cover Texts. 36bl; Paul Nasca 38b; Wikimedia Commons / Fred Hsu, March 2005; http://commons.wikimedia.org/wiki/ File:Stereogram_Tut_Random_Dot_ Shark.png Permission is granted under the terms of the GNU Free Documentation License, Version 1.2 or any later version published by the Free Software Foundation; this License, the copyright notices, and the license notice saying this License applies to the Document. 34br

All other images © Dorling Kindersley. For further information see: www.dkimages.com